Anonymous

HINDU CASTES AND SECTS

Anonymous

HINDU CASTES AND SECTS

ISBN/EAN: 9783337730796

Printed in Europe, USA, Canada, Australia, Japan

Cover: Foto ©ninafisch / pixelio.de

More available books at **www.hansebooks.com**

Hindu Castes and Sects.

AN EXPOSITION OF THE ORIGIN OF THE HINDU CASTE SYSTEM AND THE BEARING OF THE SECTS TOWARDS EACH OTHER AND TOWARDS OTHER RELIGIOUS SYSTEMS.

BY

JOGENDRA NATH BHATTACHARYA, M.A., D.L.,

President of the College of Pandits, Nadiya,
Author of "Commentaries on Hindu Law,"
"Vyavastha Kalpadruma," &c

Calcutta:
THACKER, SPINK AND CO.
1896.

[*All rights reserved.*]

CALCUTTA
PRINTED BY THACKER, SPINK AND CO.

PREFACE.

In the last edition of my "Commentaries on Hindu Law" I devoted a chapter to the Hindu Caste System which attracted the attention of the Publishers, and they suggested that the subject might well be expanded so as to be brought out as a separate volume. They suggested also that, in order to make the book complete, I should give an account not only of the Castes, but also of the important Hindu Sects, some of which are practically so many new Castes.

As I had been already engaged in writing a book about the history and philosophy of religions, the proposal, so far as the sects were concerned, was welcome indeed. About the Castes I felt very considerable diffidence; but it seemed to me that, in a town like Calcutta, where there are men from every part of India, it might not be quite impossible to collect the necessary information. When, however, I actually commenced my enquiries, then I fully realised the difficulty of my task. The original information contained in this work has been derived from a very large number of Hindu gentlemen hailing from different parts of India. I here gratefully acknowledge the kindness that they have shown in according to me their assistance. I feel very strongly inclined to insert in this book a list of their names. But the publication of such a list is not desirable for more reasons than one. To begin with, such a list would be necessarily too long to be conveniently included. Then, again, the subject of castes and sects is, in some of its aspects, a very irritating one, and if I were to give publicity to the names of the persons who have assisted me, it might place them in a very false position. So I thank them generally without mentioning any names.

In connection also with this part of the work, I must acknowledge my obligations to the works of Risley, Wilson and Sherring, and to Mr. Narsimayangar's Report of the last Census of Mysore. As to the last of these, which is compiled by an educated native of the country, it is hardly necessary to observe that it is very reliable, though not very complete. Mr. Risley's "Tribes and Castes of Bengal" is an exhaustive treatise, and is, generally speaking, reliable also. If there had been similar works for the other provinces, then the task of taking a bird's-eye view of the whole would not have been quite so arduous to me as it has actually been.

With regard to the part of the book devoted to the Hindu Sects, I may mention that the greater portion of it had been written originally for my promised work on the philosophy of religion which I hope to bring out before long. For the sake of many of my friends and relations near and dear to me I hesitated to give publicity to my views before; but it seems to me high time now that I should speak out and do what lies in me to set forth the true character of the cults that the majority of those who profess to be Hindus believe and practise.

The religions of those who are not regarded as Hindus do not come within the scope of this work. But the position which I assign to Christianity, Mahomedanism, Zoroastrianism, &c., must appear clear enough from what I have said in the Introduction to my account of the Hindu Sects, about the evolution of human faiths, and about the different principles on which they may be classified. I have tried my best throughout to avoid irreverence and offensive expressions, and the reader, who is not altogether blinded by orthodoxy, will, I hope, admit that, even with regard to the worst of the abomination-worshipping sects, I have nowhere been harsher than the nature of the case absolutely required. Reverence ought to be by all means shown to persons and institutions that have a just claim to it. But nothing can, in my opinion, be more sinful than to speak respectfully of persons who are enemies of mankind, and to whitewash rotten institutions by esoteric explanations and fine phrases.

It is no doubt extremely difficult to get rid of the effect of early training and associations. But those who claim to be educated and enlightened will, I trust, give me an impartial and patient hearing. However strong their faith in Saivism, Saktaism and Radha worship may be, they cannot be altogether blind to the real character of these creeds. One of the greatest thinkers of modern times has, in connection with certain questions of political economy, said :—

It often happens that the universal belief of one age of mankind—a belief from which no one *was*, nor, without any extraordinary effort of genius and courage, *could*, at that time be free—becomes to a subsequent age so palpable an absurdity, that the only difficulty then is to imagine how such a thing can ever have appeared credible.

This, I am sure, will before long be the feeling of every honest Hindu with regard to some of the most important features of his so-called religions, and I shall feel I have performed an almost sacred duty if this work promotes in some degree that end.

JOGENDRA NATH BHATTACHARYA.

CALCUTTA, *May* 1896.

CONTENTS.

HINDU CASTES.

PART I.

INTRODUCTION.

CHAPTER		PAGE
I.	The Origin and Nature of the Hindu Caste System	1—8
II.	Whether Caste is a Religious or a Social Distinction	9
III.	The Regulations by which the Castes have been made Exclusive	10-12
IV.	The Origin of the Additional Castes and the Sub-castes	13-15
V.	The Authorities by whom the Caste Rules are Enforced	16, 17
VI.	Nature of the Penalty of Exclusion from Caste	18

PART II.

THE BRAHMANS GENERALLY.

I.	The Position of the Brahmans in Hindu Society	19-23
II.	The Brahman's Proper Professions ...	24-26
III.	The Modern Hindu Gurus	27-29
IV.	Enquiries by which the Caste Status of a Brahman may be Ascertained ...	30-32
V.	The Sub-divisions among the Brahmans ...	33, 34

PART III.

THE BRAHMANS OF NORTHERN INDIA.

CHAPTER		PAGE
I.	The Brahmans of Bengal	35-45
	1. The Pāschātya Vaidikas	36, 37
	2. The Rārhiya Brahmans	37-42
	3. The Bārendras	42-44
	4. The Dākshinatya Vaidikas	44
	5. The Madhya Sreni Brahmans	45
II.	The Brahmans of Mithila and Behar	46-48
	1. The Maithilas	46-48
	2. The Sakaldipis	48
III.	The Brahmans of the North-Western Provinces and Oudh	49-51
	1. The Kanojias	49, 50
	2. The Sarujuparias	51
	3. The Sanadhyas	51
IV.	The Gaur Brahmans of the Kurukshetra Country	52, 53
V.	The Brahmans of Kashmir, Panjab and Sindh	54-57
	1. The Brahmans of Kashmir	54, 55
	2. The Brahmans of the Panjab	55-57
	3. The Brahmans of Sindh	57
VI.	The Brahmans of Assam	58, 59
VII.	The Brahmans of Orissa	60-64
	1. The Brahmans of Southern Orissa	60-62
	The Vaidikas	60, 61
	The Adhikari, Pujari or Vaishnava Brahmans	62
	The Mahajan Panthis	62
	The Pandas	62
	2. The Jajpuria Brahmans	63, 64
VIII.	The Brahmans of Rajputana	65-69
	1. The Srimalis	66, 67
	2. The Pallivals	68, 69
	3. The Pokaranas	69
IX.	The Brahmans of Central India	70

PART IV.

THE BRAHMANS OF SOUTHERN INDIA.

I.	Preliminary Remarks	71, 72
II.	The Brahmans of Gujrat	73-81

CHAPTER		PAGE
III.	The Brahmans of Maharashtra and Kankan	82-89
	1. The Desastha Brahmans	82, 83
	2. The Kankanasthas	83-85
	3. The Yajurvedis	85, 86
	4. The Karhades	86-89
	5. The Shenavis of Kankan	89
IV.	The Middle Class and inferior Brahmans of Maharashtra	90, 91
V.	The Brahmans of the Karnatic	92, 93
VI.	The Brahmans of Dravira	94-97
	1. The Smarta Brahmans	94, 95
	2. The Vishnuvite Brahmans of Southern India	97
VII	The Brahmans of Telingana	98-101
VIII.	The Brahmans of the Central Provinces	102, 103
IX.	The Brahmans of South Kanara	104, 105
X.	The Brahmans of Kerala, Cochin, Malabar and Travancore	106-108

PART V.

THE SEMI-BRAHMANICAL CASTES.

I.	The Bhuinhar Brahmans	109-13
II.	The Bhats and the Charauas	114-7

PART VI.

THE DEGRADED BRAHMANS.

I.	The Hossainis and Kuvachandas	118
II.	The Pirāli Tagores of Calcutta	119-124
III.	The Barna Brahmans	125, 126
IV.	The Brahmans connected with the public Shrines	127, 128
V.	The Brahmans degraded by accepting forbidden Gifts and officiating as paid Priests at Cremations	129, 130
	The Mahā-Brahmans	129
	The Agradānis	129
	The Agra Bhikshu	129
	The Sawalakhis	130

CHAPTER		PAGE
	The Bhattas	130
	The Maruiporas	130
	The Acharyas of Western India	130
	The Sanichar *alias* Dakot of Rajputana ...	130
VI.	The Brahmans degraded by Menial Service	131

PART VII.

THE MILITARY CASTES.

I.	The Rajputs	... 132-137
II.	The Kshettris	... 138-144
	1. The Sereen Kshettris ...	... 140-142
	2. Kukkurs	... 142
	3. The Rorhas	... 142
	4. The Banjai Kshettris ...	... 142-144
III.	The Jats	... 145, 146
IV.	The Khandaits of Orissa ...	... 147, 148
V.	The Marattas ...	... 149, 150
VI.	The Nairs of Malabar ...	... 151, 152
VII.	The Maravans, Ahamdians and Kallans	... 153, 154
VIII.	The Poliyas and the Koch of North Bengal.	155
IX.	The Aguris of Bengal ...	... 156-158

PART VIII.

THE SCIENTIFIC CASTES.

I.	The Vaidyas or the Medical Caste of Bengal	159-171
II.	The Bez of Assam	172
III.	The Astrologer Castes of Bengal and Assam	173, 174

PART IX.

THE WRITER CASTES.

I.	The Kāyasthas generally ...	.. 175-177
II.	The Kāyasthas of Bengal ...	.. 178-185
	1. The Dākshina Rarhis of Bengal	.. 178-180
	2. The Uttara Rarhi Kāyasthas	.. 180-183
	3. The Bangaja Kāyasthas ...	..183, 184
	4. The Bārendra Kāyasthas	184
	5. The Golam Kāyasthas of East Bengal	185

CHAPTER		PAGE
III.	The Káyasthas of Upper India	186-191
	1. The Srivatsa Káyasthas	186-188
	2. The Ambastha Káyasthas	188
	3. The Karan Káyasthas	188, 189
	4. The Sakya Seni Káyasthas	189, 190
	5. The Kula Sreshti Káyasthas	190
	6. The Bhatnagari Káyasthas	190
	7. The Mathuri Káyasthas	190
	8. The Suryadhaja Káyasthas	190
	9. The Balmiki Káyasthas	191
	10. The Ashthana Káyasthas	191
	11. The Nigama Káyasthas	191
	12. The Gaur Káyasthas	191
	13. The Káyasthas of Unao	191
IV.	The Writer Castes of Southern India	192, 193
V.	The Prabhus of the Bombay Presidency	194, 195
VI.	The Kolitas of Assam	196, 197

PART X.

THE MERCANTILE CASTES.

I.	The Baniyas of Bengal	198-202
	1. The Suvarna Baniks of Bengal	199-201
	2. The Gandha Baniks of Bengal	201, 202
II.	The Baniyas of Northern India	203-217
	1. The Agarwáls	205-207
	2. The Ossawals	207-209
	3. The Khandelwals	209, 210
	4. The Srimali Baniyas	210
	5. The Palliwal Baniyas	210
	6. The Porawal Baniyas	211
	7. The Bhatiyas	211
	8. The Mahesri Baniyas	211
	9. The Agrahari Baniyas	212
	10. The Dhunsar Baniyas	212
	11. The Umar Baniyas	212
	12. The Rastogis	213
	13, 14. The Kasarwanis and the Kasanadhans	213, 214
	15. The Lohiya Baniyas	214
	16. The Soniyas	21
	17. The Sura Senis	21
	18. The Bara Senis	214

CHAPTER			PAGE
	19. The Baranwals	... ...	215
	20. The Ayodhya Basis	... ...	215
	21. The Jaiswars	... ...	215
	22. The Mahobiyas	... ...	215
	23. The Maburis	... ...	216
	24. The Bais Baniyas	... ...	216
	25. The Kath Baniyas	... ...	216
	26. The Raoniyars	...	...216, 217
	27. The Jameyas	... ...	217
	28. The Lohanae	... ...	217
	29. The Rewaris	... ...	217
	30. The Kanus	... ...	217
III.	The Baniyas of Gujrat	... ...	218
IV.	The Trading Castes of Southern India		...219, 220
V.	The Mercantile Castes of the Telegu Country		221, 222
VI.	The Baniyas of Orissa	... ...	223

PART XI.

THE ARTISAN CASTES GENERALLY RECOGNISED AS CLEAN SUDRAS.

I.	General Observations	...	...224-226
II.	The Weavers	...	...227-236
	1. The Weavers generally	...	...227-230
	2. The Tantie of Bengal	...	...230-232
	3. The Tatwas of Behar	...	...232, 233
	4. The Kori and Koli of Upper India	...	233
	5. The Tantis of Orissa	... ...	233
	6. The Koshti of the Central Provinces		233
	7. The Weavers of Gujrat	... ...	233
	8. The Weavers of the Dravira Country		234
	9. The Weaving Castes of Mysore		...234, 235
	10. The Weavers of the Telegu Country	...	236
	11. The Jugis	... ...	236
III.	The Sweetmeat-making Castes	...	...237-239
IV.	The Kumar or Potter	... ...	240
V	The Ironsmiths	... ...	...241-243
VI.	The Goldsmiths	... ...	...244, 245
	1. The Sonar and Shakra of Northern India	... ...	...244, 245
	2. The Panchanam Varlu of the Telegu Country and the Kammallare of Dravira	... ...	245

CHAPTER		PAGE
VII.	The Carpenters	...246, 247
VIII.	The Braziers and Coppersmiths	...248, 249
	1. The Kansa Baniks of Bengal	...248, 249
	2. The Kasaras and Thatheras of Northern India	249
	3. The Gejjegora and Kanchugora of Southern India	249
IX.	The Sankha Baniks of Bengal ...	250
X.	The Grain Parchers...	...251, 252
XI.	The Dirjis or Tailors	253

PART XII.

THE MANUFACTURING AND ARTISAN CASTES THAT ARE REGARDED AS UNCLEAN SUDRAS.

I.	The Brewers, Tadi-drawers, and Sellers of Spirituous Liquors .	... 254-261
	1. The Sunris of Bengal and Behar	... 255-257
	2. The Kalwars of Northern India	...257, 258
	3. The Shanars and Illavars of Dravira	258-260
	4. The Bhándaris of Western India ...	260
	5. The Pasis of Behar ...	260
	6. The Tiyans of Southern India	261
	7. The Idigas of Mysore and the Telegu Country	261
	8. The Gaundla and Gamalla of the Telegu Country	261
II.	The Oil Manufacturers ...	... 262-264
	1. The Telis of Bengal ...	...262, 263
	2. The Kalus of Bengal ...	.. 263, 264
	3. The Telis and Ghanchis of Upper India	264
	4. The Tel Kulu Varlu of the Telegu Country	264
	5. The Ganigas and Vanikans of Southern India	264
III.	The Salt Manufacturers	265
IV.	The Leather Workers ...	... 266-268
	1. The Chamars and Muchis of N. India	266, 267
	2. The Chakilians and Madigs of S. India	267, 268
	3. The Leather-working Castes of Rajputana and Central India ...	268
V.	The Mat-makers and Basket-makers ...	269

PART XIII.

THE CLEAN AGRICULTURAL CASTES.

CHAPTER		PAGE
I.	The Kurmis and Kunbis	270-273
II.	The Koeris of Northern India	274
III.	The Malis	275, 276
IV.	The Kachis	277
V.	The Lodhas and Lodhis	278
VI.	The Agricultural Kaibartas of Bengal	279-281
VII.	The Sadgopas	282, 83
VIII.	The Agricultural Castes of the Central Provinces	284
IX.	The Agricultural Castes of the Panjab	285
X.	The Agricultural Castes of the Telegu Country	286
XI.	The Agricultural Castes of Mysore	287
XII.	The Agricultural Castes of the Dravira Country	288-290
XIII.	The Pan-growers	291-293
	1. The Barui	291, 292
	2. The Tambuli	292, 293

PART XIV.

THE COWHERDS AND SHEPHERDS.

I.	General Observations	294, 295
II.	The Abhira or Ahirs	296, 297
III.	The Gujars	298, 299
IV.	The Goalas of the Lower Provinces	300-302
V	The Cowherds of Southern India	304
VI.	The Shepherd Castes	305

PART XV.

THE CLEAN AND THE UNCLEAN CASTES EMPLOYED IN PERSONAL AND DOMESTIC SERVICE.

I.	The Barbers	306, 307
II.	The Washermen	308
III.	The Castes usually employed as Domestic Servants in Hindu Households	309
IV.	The Castes of the Domestic Servants in Anglo-Indian Households	313, 314

PART XVI.
MISCELLANEOUS CASTES.

CHAPTER		PAGE
I.	The Fishermen and Boatmen	315
II.	The Criminal Tribes	317

HINDU SECTS.

PART I.
INTRODUCTION.

I.	The Proper Method of Enquiry regarding Religions	319
II.	The Evolution of the Theocratic Art	325
III.	Classification of Religions	335
IV.	Definitions of Religion	339
V.	The True Origin of Religion	342
VI.	Religion as a Foundation of Ethics	344
VII.	General Observations about the Sect Founders	350
VIII.	The Inducements held out by Sect Founders to attract Followers	353
IX.	The Methods of Priestly Operations	353
X.	General Character of the Hindu Sects	359
XI.	Classification of the Sects	364
XII.	The Mode of ascertaining the Sect to which a Hindu Monk belongs	366

PART II.
THE SIVITE AND THE SEMI-SIVITE SECTS.

I.	The Nature of the Sivite Religion and its great Prevalence	367
II.	Probable Origin of the Sivite Religion	370
III.	The Sivite Followers of Sankara	374
IV.	The Dandis	380
V.	The Sanyasis	382
VI.	The Parama Hansas	385
VII.	The Brahmacharis	388
VIII.	The Householder Sanyasis	390
IX.	The Aghoris	391
X.	The Lingaits of Southern India	395
XI.	The Sivite Yogis	399
XII.	The Inferior Yogis	403
XIII.	The Sects that practise severe Austerities	405

PART III.

THE SAKTAS.

CHAPTER		PAGE
I.	The Nature of Sakti Worship	407
II.	The Different Classes of Saktas and their Methods of Worship	409

PART IV.

THE VISHNUVITE SECTS.

I.	The Ten Incarnations of Vishnu	414
II.	The Legends about Rama	418
III.	The Hero-god Krishna as a Historical Character	423
IV.	Krishna as the God of the modern Vishnuvite Sects	431
V.	The Sri Vaishnavas of Southern India	434
VI.	The Madhavacharis	440
VII.	The Ramanandis or Ramats of Northern India	443
VIII.	Other Ram-worshipping Sects	446
IX.	The Nimats	449
X.	The Ballavacharya Sect	451
XI.	The Chaitanite Sect of Bengal	459
XII.	The Swami Narain Sect of Gujrat	472
XIII.	Mira Bai	476
XIV.	The Mahapurushia Sect of Assam	478

PART V.

THE SEMI-VISHNUVITE AND GURU-WORSHIPPING SECTS.

I.	The Disreputable Sections of the Chaitanites		480
	1.	The Spashta Dayakas	481
	2.	The Sahajias	482
	3.	The Nara Neris	482
	4.	The Bauls	482
II.	The Disreputable Vishnuvite Sects of Upper India		484
	1.	The Radha Ballabhis	484
	2.	The Sakhi Bhavas	484

CONTENTS.

CHAPTER		PAGE
III.	The Disreputable Guru-worshipping Sects of Bengal	485
	1. The Kartabhajas ...	485
	2. The Pratapa Chandis	488
IV.	The Disreputable Guru-worshipping Sects of Upper India	490
	1. The Satnamis of Oudc	490
	2. The Paltu Dasis	491
	3. The Appa Panthis	491
	4. The Bija Margis	491
V.	The Minor Guru-worshipping Sects of Bengal	493
	1. The Bala Hari Sect	493
	2. The Kali Kumari Sect of East Bengal	494

PART VI.

MODERN RELIGIONS INTENDED TO BRING ABOUT UNION BETWEEN THE HINDUS AND THE MAHOMEDANS.

I.	The Kabir Panthis	495
II.	History of the Sikh Faith	497
III.	Nature of the Sikh Religion and its Present Condition	510

PART VII.

BUDDHISM.

I.	Personal History of Buddha	517
II.	The Rapid Spread of Buddhism and its Subsequent Disappearance from India ...	534
III.	Buddha's Religion	540
IV.	The Morality of Buddha's Religion ...	544

PART VIII.

THE JAINS.

I.	The Relative Antiquity of Jainism and Buddhism	548
II.	The Nature of the Jain Religion ...	553

HINDU CASTES AND SECTS.

PART I.
INTRODUCTION.

CHAP. I.—THE NATURE AND ORIGIN OF THE HINDU CASTE SYSTEM

THE institution of caste is a unique feature of Hindu society, and, as nothing exactly like it is to be found in any other part of the world, the manner in which it grew up in India cannot but be regarded as a question of the highest importance by the student of social phenomena. The subject has, therefore, attracted a large share of the attention of many erudite scholars, both European and Indian. The mass of information contained in their works, though not free from errors and inaccuracies, is of very great value. But the usefulness of their writings is marred, to a considerable extent, by the more or less superficial views which they take of the origin and nature of caste as a system. In speaking of it Mr. Sherring, who may be regarded as one of the chief authorities on the subject, characterises our social mechanism as "a monstrous engine of pride, dissension and shame,"* and generally has not one good word to say with reference to it or to its authors, the Brahmans. Dr. Wilson also condemns the caste system *in toto*, though in milder terms. He says that "among the Hindus the imagination of natural and positive distinction in humanity has been brought to the most fearful and pernicious development." In his dissertations on "the natural history of caste" Mr. Sherring gives, first of all, what he calls an analysis of the Brahman's character in which he finds nothing but arrogance, selfishness and ambition, and then goes on to observe:—

"To speak of the Brahmans as though they were one and the same people, with the same characteristics is delusive. For thousands of years they have been a disunited people, with mutual antipathies and non-resemblances, instead of mutual likenesses and concord. The Brahmans themselves, and none others, are responsible for this Their monstrous arrogance, selfishness and assumption have proved the bane of their race. In the cultivation of these vicious qualities they are at one, but in all other respects they are the most inharmonious and discordant people on the face of the earth.

The spread of caste, and the multiplication of separate, mutually exclusive, and inimical tribes among the lower Hindu grades, also lies at their door The detestable example they set could not but be followed by an imitative people without brains of their own. These Hindu tribes would never have dared to establish an infinity of castes among themselves without the direct sanction and assistance of the Brahmans. Moreover, when the Brahmans perceived that castes were increasing beyond decent limits, until the whole country was threatened with an endless number of caste sub-divisions, all for the most part mutually destructive, they might have peremptorily stopped their further multiplication. But they did not. On the contrary, it is plain that they looked on with the utmost satisfaction, pleased at the alienation of tribe from tribe."—Sherring's *Hindu Tribes and Castes*, Vol. III, pp. 234-35.

The inconsistencies and the fallacies abounding in these extracts are too obvious to require any critical exposition. The author's views with regard to our religion and our social polity were evidently more influenced by his zeal for his own faith of which he was a missionary, than by his sober judgment. In his lifetime he had a large number of Hindu friends who still cherish his memory with affection, and he had much better opportunities for studying the peculiarities of our

---

* See Mr. Sherring's Preface to his *Hindu Tribes and Castes*.

social fabric than most of his countrymen in India. At any rate, he may certainly be credited with having possessed sufficient knowledge of history to be aware of the shortcomings which existed in past generations, and still exist, among the priestly classes in other countries, and there can be no justification whatever for the severe censure that he has passed on the Brahmans. Yet the same views have been blindly accepted by some of the foremost of modern Hindu scholars. After stating his views regarding the probable origin of the caste system, Mr. R. C. Dutt, in his *History of India*, says :—

"It was unknown to the Hindus in the Vedic age, and was first developed in the Epic age. It divided and disunited the compact body of Aryan Hindus into three hereditary bodies, viz., the priests, the soldiers, and the people. And it permanently placed the people under the priestly and military castes; and thereby hindered popular progress and the growth of popular freedom in India.

It should be remembered, however, that with the exception of the priests and soldiers, the mass of the Hindu people still formed one united caste, the Vaishya in the Epic and succeeding ages. And the mass of the people were still entitled, like the Kshatriyas and the Brahmans, to perform sacrifices, to acquire religious knowledge, and study the Vedas. But with the loss of their independence, the Hindus have become more disunited in modern times."

The great living poet of Bengal, Babu Hem Chandra Banerji, gives countenance to similarly erroneous views, when he calls upon his countrymen to cause a clean sweep of all caste distinctions, in order that they may, by united action, recover their ancient greatness.

I am no out-and-out admirer of caste, as it exists now, and I think that, in the state of things now arising, its discipline might be relaxed in certain directions with advantage. But I believe that, generally speaking, there does not exist that antipathy between the several castes which the world at large has been led to believe. A little hitch is caused sometimes when a man of a superior caste refuses to allow one of an inferior caste to sit on the same carpet, or when the use of his waterpot is disallowed by the former to the latter. For purposes of business, not the several castes only, but even Hindus and Mahomedans can and do mix on the most friendly terms. There is, upon the whole, no more animosity between a Rajput and a Brahman than between a Rajput and a Rajput, or between a Brahman and a Brahman. If the Brahman refuses to eat in the house of a Rajput on the ground that there are no true Ksatriyas in this age of sin, the Rajput also refuses to partake of the Brahman's hospitality on the plea, afforded by the Brahmanical Shastras, that a Brahman's property should not be appropriated by a man of any caste on any account. For purposes of marriage and interchange of hospitality each caste is an independent and exclusive body, and all the classes are placed on a coequal footing. Such being the case, the so-called inferior castes show no more eagerness to be enrolled among the higher, than the latter do to be reduced to the level of the former. It is open to the lower castes to practise any profession, excepting that of a priest, and as every Hindu has a recognized position within his own caste, which does not vary with any viscissitude of fortune, no one can feel inclined to crush out that system, and run the risk of losing its certain advantages, for the uncertain prospect of acquiring a better social footing by working as it were upon a *tabula rasa*. A few low caste parvenus there may be, who, in their innermost hearts, feel ashamed of even their own parents and brothers. But the aspirations of these men certainly do not deserve much sympathy. Generally speaking, the Hindus look upon the several divisions in their society as the necessary component parts of their social mechanism, and there can be no occasion for jealousy or bitter feelings.

' Caste has had its origin, no doubt, in Brahmanical legislation. But there is no ground whatever for the doctrine that it is the outcome of the policy embodied in the Machiavelian maxim *Divide and Rule*. A very little reflection ought to show that the caste system, introduced and enforced by the Brahminical Shastras, could not possibly be the cause of any social split. On the contrary, it provided bonds of union between races and clans that had nothing in common before its introduction. There is no ground whatever for the supposition that in primitive India all classes of people were united as one man, and that the "unnatural and pernicious caste system" was forced on them by the Brahmans with the diabolical object of sowing dissensions among them. The more correct view seems to be that the legislation of the Rishis was calculated not only to bring about union between the isolated clans that lived in primitive India, but to render it possible to assimilate within each group the foreign hordes that were expected to pour into the country from time to time. If those Englishmen who have permanently settled in this country recognized the sacredness of the Shastras, and refrained from eating forbidden food, they might be admitted into the Ksatriya clan under the name of Sakya Seni Rajputs. The authors of such legislation deserve certainly to be admired for their large-hearted statesmanship, instead of being censured for selfish ambition and narrowness.

The ambition that led the Hindu lawgivers to place their own class above the rest of mankind, has, no doubt, an appearance of selfishness. But if self-aggrandisement had been, as is alleged, their sole motive, then there was nothing to prevent them from laying down the law that the proper men to enjoy the kingly office and the various loaves and fishes of the public service, were the Brahmans. The highest secular ambition of the Brahman was to be the unpaid adviser of the Crown, and, as a matter of actual practice, the entire civil service was left by them in the hands of the Kāyasthas. Such professions, accompanied by such conduct, do not betray selfishness. It was only in respect of matters relating to religion that the Brahmans kept in their hands the monopoly of power. But they could not have taken any other course without upsetting altogether the fabric which they had built up.

Circumstanced as India, presumably, was in ancient times, there could not possibly have been in that state of things, any great attraction either for military service or for intellectual pursuits. The resources of the country were then too limited for adequately rewarding either the soldier or the scholar, and as any able-bodied man could, in those times, earn his living without any difficulty, either in agricultural pursuits or by breeding cattle, the only way to induce any class of men to adopt a more ambitious or risky career, lay in giving them a superior status by hereditary right. The importance of the service which caste has done to India may be realized, to some extent, from the fact that when, in a party of Hindus, comments are made about an illiterate Brahman, an unbusiness like Kāyastha or a cowardly Ksatriya, they not unfrequently express their doubt as to his very legitimacy. Such being the case, no Kshatriya can refuse to fight, when there is occasion, without laying himself open to the most galling of reproaches. His ancestors never shrank from legitimate fighting, and so he has no choice left.

"He too would rather die than shame."

It is feeling of this kind that urged the ancient Ksatriyas to desperate deeds for the defence of their country, and though long since fallen, yet modern history is not altogether wanting in testimony as to the greatness of that mighty race. The name of Babu Kumāra Sing, the last great Rajput hero, is not likely to be soon forgotten, though English historians may not do him justice. Goaded on to rebellion by the ungenerous suspicions entertained against him by a local official, and by the attempt made by that official to insult and imprison him, he besought his friends, relatives and adherents, to remain loyal to the British Government, and to leave him to shift for himself. But he was the idol of the Bhojpuriās, and they gathered round him, like one man, to fight under his banner. At their head the octogenarian hero fought bravely to the last, and displayed throughout far better generalship and valour than the cowards who took the leading part in bringing about the conflagration. The old Rajput baron knew well that he had no chance of ultimate success. But as a Ksatriya, claiming the blood of the great Vikramaditya in his veins, he could not submit to die like a traitor on the scaffold. Had the Government of Bengal reposed that confidence in him which he certainly deserved, the whole province of Behar would probably have remained as quiet as Bengal, and the operations of the mutineers would have been confined to the North-West Provinces and Oude only.

In their fourfold division of caste, the Rishis placed their own class, *i.e.*, the descendants of the Vedic singers and their comrades, above all the others. To the fighting classes the Brahmanical codes assigned the second rank, and the process, by which they were reconciled to accept the position that was given them, is replete with interest. With regard to the superiority of the Brahmans, Manu says :—

"Since the Brahman sprang from the most excellent part, since he was the first born, and since he possesses the Veda, he is by right the chief of this whole creation."—Manu, I, 93.

But while thus glorifying the Brahmans, the Rishis made great concessions to the Ksatriyas by declaring that the office of the king was their birthright, and also by enjoining on all classes the duty of implicit obedience to the king.

Brahmanical legislation has been very successful in organising the Brahman and the Ksatriya castes. To a very great extent, the descendants of the Vedic singers and their comrades have become one race under the name of Brahmans. To a still greater extent have the several fighting clans recognized each other as members of one great family, under the name of Ksatriyas or Rajputs. The Vaishya caste was, in all probability, never successfully formed, and, so far as this class is concerned, Brahmanical legislation failed to attain its very noble object. The Baniyas who practise trade and are, generally speaking, a wealthy class, claim in some places to be Vaishyas. But, in all probability, the majority of the traders, artisans, and agriculturists never cared for the honour of being invested with the sacred thread, or for the privilege of reading the Vedas. And when such was the case, the Brahmans themselves could not be too anxious to force these honours and privileges upon them. The chief concern of the Brahmans, in the efforts they made to realise their ideal of social polity, was to keep the fighting clans in good humour, so that even if the Vaishyas sought for the honour of the thread, the Brahmans could not have given it to them without depriving it of thevalue which it came to acquire in the eyes of the Ksatriyas.

Caste is often described by European scholars as an iron chain which has fettered each class to the profession of their ancestors, and has rendered any improvement on their part impossible. This view may, to some extent, be regarded as correct so far as the lower classes are concerned. But with regard to the higher classes, caste is a golden chain which they have willingly placed around their necks, and which has fixed them to only that which is noble and praiseworthy. Any little split that is caused by caste now and then is far outweighed by the union of races and clans which it has promoted and fostered, and there is no justification whatever for the abuse which has been heaped upon its authors.

CHAP. II.—WHETHER CASTE IS A SOCIAL, OR A RELIGIOUS DISTINCTION?

The question has been hotly discussed, whether caste is a social or a religious distinction? As shown in the last chapter, it is mainly a social distinction. But as many of the ordinances of our Shastras are based upon it, it has a religious aspect also. The religious rights and duties of the Hindus do in fact vary, to a considerable extent, according to their caste. For instance, on the death of an agnate within seven degrees, a Brahman has to observe mourning for ten days only, while a man of the fighting caste has to wear the "weeds of woe" for twelve days, a man of the mercantile caste for fifteen days, and a Sudra for one full month. Then, again, the Vedic rites and prayers which the three higher castes are required to perform every day are all prohibited to the Sudra. The latter can be taught to repeat only those prayers that are prescribed by what may be called the new testaments of the Hindus, *i.e.*, the Purāns and the Tāntras. But the Brahman who enlists even a good Sudra among his disciples is lowered for ever in the estimation of the people, while by ministering to a Sudra of a low class he is degraded altogether.

CHAP. III.—THE REGULATIONS BY WHICH THE CASTES HAVE BEEN MADE EXCLUSIVE.

THE rules defining the proper avocations of the several castes are not imperative, it being laid down in the Shastras that a person, unable to earn his livelihood otherwise, may take to a profession which is ordinarily prohibited to his class. Manu says :—

80. "Among the several occupations *for gaining a livelihood* the most commendable respectively for the sacerdotal, military, and mercantile classes, are teaching the Veda, defending, and commerce or keeping herds and flocks.

81. Yet a Brahman unable to subsist by his duties just mentioned may live by the duty of a soldier, for that is the next in rank.

82. If it be asked, how he must live, should he be unable to get a subsistence by either of these employments, *the answer is*, he may subsist as a mercantile man, applying himself *in person* to tillage and attendance on cattle.

95. A military man in distress may subsist by all these means, but at no time must he have recourse to the highest, *or sacerdotal* function.

98. A mercantile man, unable to subsist by his own duties, may descend even to the servile acts of a Sudra, taking care never to do what ought never to be done; but, when he has gained a competence, let him depart from service.

99. A man of the fourth class, not finding employment by waiting on the twice-born, while his wife and son are tormented with hunger, may subsist by handicrafts.—Manu, *Chap. X.*"

Such being the precepts of the Shastras, it is very often found that a Hindu of one class is engaged in a profession which is the speciality of another, and the tendency of English education is to make all the castes more and more regardless about strict compliance with Shastric rules on the subject. The Hindu legislators made the castes exclusive, not so much by prescribing particular professions for each, as by prohibiting intermarriage and interchange of hospitality on a footing of equality. In the beginning intermarriage was allowed so far that a man of a superior caste could lawfully take in marriage a girl of an inferior caste. But, by what may be called the Hindu new testaments, intermarriage between the different castes is prohibited altogether. As to interchange of hospitality, the Shastras lay down that a Brahman must avoid, if possible, the eating of any kind of food in the house of a Sudra, and that under no circumstances is he to eat any food cooked with water and salt by a Sudra, or touched by a Sudra after being so cooked. In practice the lower classes of Brahmans are sometimes compelled by indigence to honour the Sudras by accepting their hospitality—of course, eating only uncooked food or such food as is cooked by Brahmans with materials supplied by the host. The prejudice against eating cooked food that has been touched by a man of an inferior caste is so strong that, although the Shastras do not prohibit the eating of food cooked by a Ksatriya or Vaishya, yet the Brahmans, in most parts of the country, would not eat such food. For these reasons, every Hindu household—whether Brahman, Ksatriya or Sudra—that can afford to keep a paid cook generally entertains the services of a Brahman for the performance of its *cuisine*—the result being that, in the larger towns, the very name of Brahman has suffered a strange degradation of late, so as to mean only a cook.

The most important regulations by which the castes have been made exclusive are those which relate to marriage. In fact, as Mr. Risley in his valuable work on the *Castes and Tribes of Bengal* rightly observes, "caste is a matter mainly relating to marriage." Matrimonial alliances out of caste is prevented by the seclusion of the females, their early marriage, and the social etiquette which requires that even the marriages of boys should be arranged for them by their parents or other guardians. The Hindu youth has to maintain an attitude of utter indifference about every proposal regarding his marriage, and when any arrangement in that respect is made by his parents, grand-parents, uncles or elder brothers, he has to go through the ceremony out of his sense of duty to obey or oblige them. The selection being, in all cases, made by the guardian in accordance with his sober judgment, and never by the parties themselves in accordance with their impulses for the time being, marriage out of caste is almost impossible in Hindu society, and is never known to take place except among the very lowest.

CHAP. IV.—THE ORIGIN OF THE ADDITIONAL CASTES AND THE SUB-CASTES.

THE sentiments which Brahmanical legislation engendered and fostered have led to the formation or recognition of a vast number of extra castes and sub-castes. In all probability the laws of the Shastras failed to bring about a complete fusion of all the clans and races that had been intended to be included within the same group, and their recognition, as distinct subdivisions, was inevitable from the very beginning. New sub-divisions have also been formed in later times by the operation of one or other of the following causes :—

1. By migration to different parts of the country.
2. By different sections being devoted to the practice of distinct professions.
3. By any section being elevated above or degraded below the level of the others.
4. By quarrels between the different sections of the same caste as to their relative status.
5. By becoming the followers of one of the modern religious teachers.
6. By the multiplication of the illegitimate progeny of religious mendicants.

The Brahmanical sub-classes like the Rādhis, Bārendras and the Kanojias are so-called on account of their being the inhabitants of Rādh, Bārendra, and Kanoj, though they all belong to the same stock. The Vaidikas are evidently so-called on account of their devoting themselves exclusively to the study and the teaching of the Vedas. If so, then it is not difficult to see why they kept themselves aloof from those who pursued secular avocations. The Husainis, Kalankis Mahā-Brahmans, Agradānis, Sanicharis, Gangāputras, &c., have become more or less exclusive by being degraded and debarred from association with the other classes of Brahmans on a footing of equality. When one section of a caste affect a superior status and refuse to give their daughters to another section, the latter may for a time admit their inferiority by betraying an eagerness to marry their daughters in the superior caste without having the compliment reciprocated. But sooner or later the connection between them is cut off altogether, and they become distinct sub-castes. With regard to the additional castes, it is stated in the Shastras that they are due to intermarriage and miscegenation between the primary castes. This explanation is necessitated by the theory that originally there were only four castes and has been of great use to the Brahmans for enforcing marriage within caste, and for humiliating such classes as the Vaidyas and the Acharyas who, being by the nature of their profession, very important factors in every native court, might otherwise have become too powerful.

To me it seems that most of the so-called "mixed castes" owe their exclusiveness to either Brahmanical policy, or to the impossibility of including them within any of the four primary groups; while there are some among the additional castes whose formation is clearly traceable to their being the followers of some revolutionary teacher of modern times.

The Brahmanical explanation of the origin of the additional castes has been accepted by some of the English writers on the subject. But to me it seems utterly impossible that any new caste could be formed in the manner described by Manu or any other Hindu lawgiver. In order to accept the theory it is necessary to assume that a careful record was kept of every case of irregular marriage and illicit sexual intercourse, and that the progeny of the parties were listed and included under separate groups by royal edicts. What seems much more probable is, that in order to make the primary divisions into four castes practically acceptable, most of the sub-divisions in each of them had to be recognized at the very beginning, and the tendency which was thus generated received further expansion by the recognition of the additional castes on account of the circumstances and reasons mentioned already. The motives that led the Brahmans to declare that the astrologer was the son of a shoemaker, and that the medical men were the offspring of irregular marriage between a Brahman and a Vaishya woman, ought to be clear enough to every one who has any idea of the intrigues that usually prevailed in the courts of the Hindu kings.

CHAP. V.—THE AUTHORITIES BY WHOM CASTE RULES ARE ENFORCED.

UNDER the Hindu kings, the rules relating to caste were enforced by the officers of the crown in accordance with the advice of the great Pandits who generally acted as ministers. During the period of Moslem ascendancy, the Hindu barons and chiefs exercised the prerogative where they could. But in Northern India, the Hindus have now no recognised spiritual head. In cases of serious violations of Shastric injunctions, the Pandits are consulted as to the nature of the expiation required. But their power to impose any penalty on the delinquent is not very considerable. In extreme cases they may, as a body, refuse to accept any gift from the offender, and keep aloof from the religious ceremonies celebrated in his house. But except where public opinion is too strong to be disregarded, they are very seldom sufficiently united to visit anyone with the punishment of excommunication in such manner.

In Southern India the case is somewhat different. There the non-Vishnuvite Hindus are completely under the spiritual authority of the Superiors of the Sankarite monasteries. In fact, the head of the Sringeri monastery, at the source of the Toonga Bhadra in Mysore, has the same power over the Smarta Hindus of Southern India that the Pope has over the Roman Catholic population of Europe. See *The Queen* v. *Sri Sankara*, I. L. R., 6 Madras, p. 381.

The main agency by which caste discipline is still maintained to some extent is the religious sentimentalism of the Hindus as a nation. But in this respect there is no consistency to be found in them. For instance, there are lots of men who almost openly eat forbidden food and drink forbidden liquors, and yet their fellow-castemen do not usually hesitate to dine in their houses, or to have connections with them by marriage. But if a man goes to Europe he loses his caste, even though he be a strict vegetarian and teetotaler. Then, again, if a man marry a widow he loses caste, though such marriage is not in any way against Shastric injunctions, while the keeping of a Mahomedan mistress, which is a serious and almost inexpiable offence, is not visited with any kind of punishment by castemen. Similarly, a man may become a Brahmo or agnostic and yet remain in caste; but if he espouse Christianity or Mahomedanism, his own parents would exclude him from their house, and disallow every kind of intercourse, except on the most distant terms. He cannot have even a drink of water under his parental roof, except in an earthen pot, which would not be touched afterwards by even the servants of the house, and which he would have to throw away with his own hands, if no scavenger be available.

The only acts which now lead to exclusion from caste are the following :—

1. Embracing Christianity or Mahomedanism.
2. Going to Europe or America.
3. Marrying a widow.
4. Publicly throwing away the sacred thread.
5. Publicly eating beef, pork or fowl.
6. Publicly eating *kachi* food cooked by a Mahomedan, Christian or low caste Hindu.
7. Officiating as a priest in the house of a very low class Sudra.
8. By a female going away from home for an immoral purpose.
9. By a widow becoming pregnant.

In the villages, the friendless and the poor people are sometimes excluded from caste for other offences as, for instance :—adultery, incest, eating forbidden food and drinking forbidden liquors. But when the offender is an influential personage or is influentially connected, no one thinks of visiting him with such punishment.

CHAP. VI.—NATURE OF THE PENALTY OF EXCLUSION FROM CASTE.

WHEN a Hindu is excluded from caste—

1. His friends, relatives and fellow-townsmen refuse to partake of his hospitality.
2. He is not invited to entertainments in their houses.
3. He cannot obtain brides or bridegrooms for his children.
4. Even his own married daughters cannot visit him without running the risk of being excluded from caste.
5. His priest and even his barber and washerman refuse to serve him.
6. His fellow-castemen sever their connection with him so completely that they refuse to assist him even at the funeral of a member of his household.
7. In some cases the man excluded from caste is debarred access to the public temples.

To deprive a man of the services of his barber and washerman is becoming more and more difficult in these days. But the other penalties are (enforced on excluded persons) with more or less rigour, according to circumstances.

In the mofussil the penalties are most severely felt. Even in the towns such persons find great difficulty in marrying their children, and are therefore sometimes obliged to go through very humiliating expiatory ceremonies, and to pay heavy fees to the learned Pandits for winning their good graces.

PART II.
THE BRAHMANS GENERALLY.

CHAP I.—THE POSITION OF THE BRAHMANS IN HINDU SOCIETY

THE most remarkable feature in the mechanism of Hindu society is the high position occupied in it by the Brahmans. They not only claim almost divine honours as their birthright, but, generally speaking, the other classes, including the great Ksatriya princes, and the rich Vaishya merchants readily submit to their pretensions as a matter of course. A Brahman never bows his head to make a *pranam* to one who is not a Brahman. When saluted by a man of any other class, he only pronounces a benediction saying, " Victory be unto you." In some cases when the party saluting is a prince or a man of exalted position in society, the Brahman, in pronouncing his benediction, stretches out the palm of his right hand, in a horizontal direction, to indicate that he has been propitiated. The form of salutation by the inferior castes to Brahmans varies according to circumstances. When the Brahman to be saluted has a very high position, temporal or spiritual, and the man saluting desires to honour him to the utmost degree possible, he falls prostrate at the feet of the object of his reverence, and, after touching them with his hand applies his fingers to his lips and his forehead. In ordinary cases a man, of any of the three inferior castes, salutes a Brahman by either joining his palms and raising them to his forehead, in the form of a double military salute, or by simply pronouncing such words as *pranam* or *paunlagi*. Thus the amount of veneration shown to a Brahman may vary under different conditions. But no member of the other castes can, consistently with Hindu social etiquette and religious beliefs, refuse altogether to bow to a Brahman. Even the Chaitanites and the other classes of modern Vaishnavas, who do not profess to have any veneration for the Brahmans as such, and speak of them as heretics in their own circle, cannot do without bowing to Brahmans and accepting their benedictions in public.

The more orthodox Sudras carry their veneration for the priestly class to such an extent, that they will not cross the shadow of a Brahman, and it is not unusual for them to be under a vow not to eat any food in the morning, before drinking Bipracharanāmrita, *i.e.*, water in which the toe of a Brahman has been dipped. On the other hand, the pride of the Brahman is such that they do not bow to even the images of the gods worshipped in a Sudra's house by Brahman priests.

The Brahman asserts his superiority in various other ways. His Shastras declare that on certain occasions, Brahmans must be fed and gifts must be made to them by members of all classes. But the Brahman can accept such hospitality and gifts without hesitation only where the host or donor is a member of one of the three superior castes. The position of the Sudras is, according to the theory of the Shastras and the practice of Hindu society such, that a Brahman cannot accept their presents without lowering himself for ever, while by eating any kind of food cooked by a Sudra he loses his Brahmanism and his sanctity altogether. In the house of a Sudra, a Brahman may eat uncooked food, or such food as is cooked by a Brahman. But the Brahman who does so, while not sojourning in a foreign place, is lowered for ever in public estimation. For all these reasons, a Brahman who accepts a Sudra's gifts and hospitality at a religious ceremony, is able to pose as a person who makes a great sacrifice to oblige the host and donor.

When a Brahman invites a Sudra, the latter is usually asked to partake of the host's *prasāda*, or favour, in the shape of the leavings of his plate. Orthodox Sudras actually take offence, if invited by the use of any other formula. No Sudra is allowed to eat in the same room or at the same time with Brahmans. While the Brahman guests eat, the Sudras have to wait in a different part of the house. It is not, however, to be supposed that the Sudras take any offence at such treatment. On the contrary, they not only wait patiently, but, in some places, insist upon eating the leavings of the Brahmans, and refuse to eat anything from clean plates. Such orthodoxy is against nature, and is happily somewhat rare. Ordinarily, the pious Sudra takes a pinch from the leavings of a Brahman's plate, and after eating the same with due reverence, begins to eat from a clean plate.

The high caste and well-to-do Sudras never eat in the house of a Brahman without paying for the honour a *pranami*, or salutation fee, of at least one rupee. The Brahman host never insists on such payment, and in fact it is usually forced upon him. But when a Brahman eats in the house of a Sudra on a ceremonial occasion, the payment of a fee by the host to the guest is a *sine qua non*. This fee is called *bhojan dakshina*, and ordinarily varies from one anna to one rupee. In special cases the Sudra host has to pay much heavier fees.

When a Sudra writes a letter to a Brahman, it must begin by declaring that the writer makes a hundred million obeisances at the lotus feet of the addressee. When a Brahman writes a letter to a man of any other caste, the style of his communication is that of a superior being, and he commences it by pouring "heaps of assurances of future bliss."

If the amount of honour which is shewn by any community to its female members is an indication of the degree of civilization attained by it, then, the Brahmans are, the most advanced race of men on earth. They never mention the names of their ladies without the affix *devi* (goddess). But while thus upholding the dignity of the female members of their own class, they have taught the Sudras to use the word *dasi* (slave) as an affix to the names of Sudra females.

For conversational purposes the proper form of address by Sudras to Brahmans is Thākoor Mahasaya or Thākoorji which means "venerable god." In the same way Brahman ladies have to be addressed by Sudras as Ma Thākoorain or mother goddess. Formerly, even the Brahman kings of the country preferred the address of Thākoor to any other honorific expression. But of late years the word has suffered a strange degradation, and though it means "god" it is now very often taken to denote a cook.* For this reason the Brahmans who have received an English education, and are engaged in secular pursuits, saw no objection at one time to be addressed as Babus. But the epithet, Babu itself, has suffered of late a similar degradation. Before the commencement of British rule, it was applied only to the collateral relatives of the great royal families of India. But Englishmen in India applied it indiscriminately to every untitled Hindu, and specially to their Hindu clerks in Bengal. The title is, therefore, now usually taken to be the equivalent of the English words, "clerk" and "accountant," and the higher classes of educated Hindus now consider it an insult to be called Babus. In the absence of any other Indian word for honorific address, some Hindu gentlemen now prefer to be addressed as "Mr." and "Esquire," and for this they

---

* See p. 11, *ante*.

are found fault with and ridiculed, both by their countrymen and foreigners. But the fact is that the Hindu titles have suffered such degradation of late, that the untitled aristocracy of the country are compelled by sheer necessity to assume other epithets. If the word Thākoor retained its original signification, surely no Brahman, however exalted his secular position might be, would feel ashamed of that glorious honorific, or prefer the foreign epithets "Mr" and "Esquire."

CHAP. II.—THE BRAHMAN'S PROPER PROFESSIONS.

ACCORDING to the commandments of his religion, the proper avocations of Brahmans are the following :—

1. Studying the Shastras.
2. Teaching the Shastras.
3. Performance of religious rites for the three superior classes.
4. Acceptance of gifts from the three superior classes.

Until recently the teaching of the Shastras was considered as the most honourable profession for a Brahman. The great Pandits of the country are still honoured and subsidized by the well-to-do classes. But their pretensions to superior learning are not admitted by those who have received an English education, and as their vaunted lore does not open the doors to any kind of service under Government, or to the liberal professions, they are fast sinking to a very inferior position. There was a time when the first Pandit in the country was the first man in the country. The people believed in the Pandits and, under the Hindu kings, the entire administration was very often left in their hands. But under British rule, the Pandits are nowhere. They still exercise very considerable influence over the uneducated classes. But the dignity of their profession is gone, and the class itself is fast becoming extinct in consequence of the superior attractions of English education.

As to the priestly profession, it is to be observed that the ordinance which recommends it as a proper one for a Brahman, is subject to very important limitations. Those who officiate as priests for Sudras, and those who perform the service of idols in public or private shrines, are, according to the dogmas of the Hindu scriptures, degraded persons. The performance of priestly functions for the superior castes is nowhere condemned in the sacred codes, and is, in fact, recommended as a proper avocation for a Brahman. But, according to Hindu notions, a priest is a very inferior person, and no Brahman, who can live otherwise, would willingly perform the work of a priest. The duties of the Brahman pastor involve long fastings, and, in respect of the worship of idols, almost menial service. Further, the men who actually perform the function of priests are, in the majority of cases, ignorant persons with just the amount of the knowledge of rituals that is necessary for discharging their duties. The Pandits, who study the original works that regulate these rituals, can find fault with the priest at every step, and reserve for themselves the higher functions of the critic and superintendent.

Whatever be the reason, the priest has a very inferior position in Hindu society. The relative status of Brahman families depends partly upon the hereditary rank of its members, as determined by the records of Indian heraldry. But, apart from aristocratic lineage, the highest position among the Brahmans is, according to orthodox notions, occupied by the Pandits and the Gurus who have only Brahman disciples. The Gurus are principally of two classes—namely, Tāntric and Vaishnava. The Tāntric Gurus inculcate mainly the worship of Siva's consorts; while the Vaishnava Gurus or Gossains insist upon the worship of one of the incarnations of Vishnu. The disciples of the Gossains are men of very low castes, including vintners, oilmen, and even the "unfortunates" of the towns. Having such followers, the Gossains are a very well-to-do class, but are held in very low esteem, and very few good Brahmans eat in their houses.

Among the Tāntric Gurus there are a great many who have only Brahman disciples. They are generally very learned men, and are not like the Vaishnava Gossains, who are usually so illiterate that the few among them who can barely recite the Sri Bhāgavat are reckoned by their followers as prodigies of Sanskrit scholarship.

CHAP III.—THE MODERN HINDU GURUS.

A FEW words about the probable origin of the modern Guru's profession may not be out of place here. There is no mention of it in the ancient scriptures of the Hindus, and it is recognized and regulated only by their new testaments. The word Guru or Acharya originally meant a teacher of the Vedas. The ancient legal and moral codes of the Hindus gave a very high position to the Vedic teachers. Manu says :—

"Of him who gives natural birth, and him who gives knowledge of the whole Veda, the giver of sacred knowledge is the more venerable father, since the second or divine birth ensures life to the twice-born, both in this world and hereafter eternally."—Manu II, 146.

When, by such teachings, the position of the Guru became associated in the Hindu mind with the tenderest sentiments of regard and affection, the Brahmanical theologians began to think of devising ways to exact that reverence even from persons who have never been Vedic pupils, and who have not even the right to read our holy scriptures. The Vedic mantras are too voluminous and prosaic to attract any considerable number of pupils. Females and Sudras are not allowed to study them at all. For these reasons, no actual teacher of the Vedas could at any time hope to attract round him any considerable number of actual Vedic students. But the position of a Guru having a large number of pupils is a desirable one, and the Tāntrics invented a short cut to that position. They gave the name mantra to some mystic and meaningless syllables which might be communicated and learnt at one sitting. Sudras and females were made eligible for these mantras, and every Brahman with a little tact and show of piety was enabled to gather round him an army of *chellas* bound by their vow to worship him as a god and to pay a yearly tax to him and his descendants from generation to generation. The *chellas* are regarded by the Guru as his property, and when the sons of a deceased Guru make a partition of his estate and effects, the *chellas* are partitioned and distributed among them in the same manner as any other property inherited by them.

The simple method invented by the Tāntrics for acquiring the power and position of a Guru over a large number of disciples, has been remarkably successful. Looked at *à priori* such mystic syllables as *hoong*, *doong*, *kling* or *hring* are an outrage on common sense. But the gullibility of man has no limit, and the Guru who whispers these meaningless expressions in the ears of his disciple is worshipped and paid by him as the bestower of untold benefits. He is not allowed to reveal its nature to any one. The matter is certainly not such as to be capable of bearing the daylight of intelligent criticism. The Guru, therefore, acts wisely in insisting that the communication should be treated as strictly confidential.

The Gossains discard the mystic syllables more or less, and inculcate that in this age of sin the only way to attain salvation lies in constantly repeating the name of *Hari!* Their doctrine may not at first sight seem to be consistent with their professional policy. A Tāntric mantra is a mystic syllable which must necessarily be received from a Guru by those who may value it. But if, as the Vishnuvites say, a man can save his soul by merely repeating the name of some deity a certain number of times, surely he cannot be absolutely in need of a spiritual teacher to initiate him in the adoption of that method. But logic or reason has very little connection with faith, and as Gurus of all classes, including both the Tāntric and the Vaishnava, insist upon the necessity of a spiritual teacher for every human being, the idea has become too firmly implanted in the Hindu mind to be eradicated by any occasional gleam of common sense.

The abominations worshipped by the Tāntrics are eschewed altogether by the Vaishnavas. But the latter by reciting stories or singing songs about the illicit amours of Krishna, gives perhaps greater encouragement to immorality than any Tāntric the nature of whose phallic emblems is understood by very few of those who worship them. So there is very little to choose between the morality of the one or the other. But the Vaishnavas can perform their operations openly, while the Tāntrics require a shroud of mysticism to envelop them. Anyhow, the Vaishnavas are very fast extending the sphere of their influence, and many of the Tāntrics are now espousing Vaishnava tenets in order to have the advantage of enlisting among their followers the low classes that are becoming rich under British rule.

CHAP. IV —ENQUIRIES BY WHICH THE CASTE STATUS OF A HINDU MAY BE ASCERTAINED.

CANNOT a man of one caste pass* as a member of another caste? This is a question which must occur to every foreigner interesting himself in the subject. But, as explained already, there cannot be any strong motive for such false impersonation, and the checks which are provided by Hindu social etiquette, are powerful enough to repress any such attempts. The unwritten law of Indian society requires that every Hindu, when asked, must mention not only the names of his paternal and maternal ancestors, but give also every information that he can about such queries as the following :—

1. What is your caste?
2. What is your clan?
3. What is your Gotra?
4. What are your Pravaras?
5. What is your Veda?
6. What is your Sákha?
7. What is your Sutra?

---

* I once heard a story about an attempt made by a shoemaker to pass as a Brahman. With a view to have a share of the nice eatables provided for the Brahman guests of a local Dives, he equipped himself like a Brahman with his sacred thread, and quietly joined the company when they assembled in the evening. As usual on such occasions, one of the party asked him what his name and his father's name were. He said, in reply, that his own name was Ram Chatterjea, and that his father's name was Kasi Lahiri. Being thus found out, he was hustled out of the place. His low position in caste saved him from kicks and blows, and while effecting his exit he gave expression to the sad moral of his adventure by muttering "a shoemaker cannot conceal his caste even under cover of night."

There are also special enquiries for each caste and clan, and these go into such details that it must be quite impossible for an outsider to answer them. I shall refer to some of those details further on, but it seems to me absolutely necessary to give some information about Gotra, Pravara, &c., in this place.

Gotra.—The Gotra of a Brahman is the name of the Rishi or Vedic poet from whom he and his agnates are supposed to be descended. The Gotra of a man of any other caste is the name of the Rishi who and whose descendants were entitled to officiate as priests in the family of his ancestors. The original meaning of the word was, in all probability, a place for keeping cattle. But, with the highest possible respect for the authority of Professor Max Müller, I see no reason whatever to suppose that the Brahmans, Rajputs and Vaishyas, who now profess to be of the same Gotra, have this tradition, because their ancestors lived within the same cow-pen. In the vernacular languages of India, the word *got* means simply a company of men, and the authority of the Shastras is distinctly in favour of the view that the men who profess to be of the same Gotra, are either the actual descendants, or the progeny of the spiritual sons of the same primitive priest. The origin of the Gotra is to be traced not to actual residence within the same cow-pen, but to a metaphorical use of the word similar to that which is made of the term 'flock' by the priests of the Christian Church.

Pravara.—The word literally means a person duly appointed. On the view which I take of the *Gotra*, the Pravaras of a Hindu are the Rishis who were entitled to be appointed as assistant priests for the performance of the religious ceremonies of his ancestors. On any other view the *Pravaras* can have no meaning whatever.

Vedas and Sākha.—Every Brahman is supposed to be a reader of one of the four Vedas, and though the study has, for various reasons, been suppressed long since, yet every member of the priestly caste is expected to know by tradition the name of the Veda, and the rescension of it of which his family profess to be students. Hence, when any enquiry is made about the lineage of any member of the twice-born castes, he is asked to mention the name of his Veda.

Sutra.—The Sutras are ritualistic works, and the Sutra of a Brahman is the name of the Rishi whose manual of rituals regulates the religious ceremonies of his family. Every Brahman in the country is supposed to know his Gotra, Pravara and Veda, and is expected to mention them whenever asked. But the Sākha and the Sutra are known only to the learned, and it is not very usual to make any enquiry about them even on formal occasions.

A difference of Gotra, Pravara, Vedas or Sākha does not usually imply any difference of caste or clan ; nor does any identity in these respects imply an identity of class. There is a saying in Bengali according to which there are only five Gotras in the world. As a matter of fact there are more than 100 different Gotras, and each one of these is to be found in almost all the primary castes. The Gotra is not only something very different from caste, but involves very opposite incidents. The most important feature of caste is that no Hindu can contract a marital alliance outside its limits. But as to Gotra the rule among the higher castes is that marriage can only be valid between persons of different Gotra.

CHAP. V.—THE SUB-DIVISIONS AMONG THE BRAHMANS

ACCORDING to some authoritative texts of the Shastras, and according to popular belief also, the Brahmans of India are divided into two main classes, each of them being sub-divided into five sub-classes as shown in the following table :—

1. Panch Gaur or the five classes of Northern India.
   1. Sarswata.
   2. Kanya Kubja.
   3. Gaudra.
   4. Utkala.
   5. Maithila.

2. Panch Dravira or the five classes of Southern India.
   1. Maharashtra.
   2. Andra.
   3. Dravira.
   4. Carnata.
   5. Guzrat.

As a matter of fact the divisions among the Brahmans are so numerous that it is exceedingly difficult, if not actually impossible, to frame an exhaustive and accurate list thereof. For the purpose of giving an account of the Brahmans of Northern India alone, each of the following provinces and districts must be taken into consideration separately: (1) Bengal Proper ; (2) Tirhoot ; (3) South Behar ; (4) N.-W. Provinces and Oudh ; (5) Kurukshetra ; (6) Punjab ; (7) Kashmir ; (8) Sind ; (9) Rajputana ; (10) Central India ; (11) Assam ; (12) Orissa.

Even within the limits of each of the above-mentioned territorial divisions, the Brahmanical population are not, in any case, of the same class. In Bengal proper alone, there are, besides the degraded and the semi-degraded Brahmans, about half-a-dozen different divisions in the sacerdotal population which are, for all practical purposes, different castes altogether. The case is no better in any of the other provinces. On the contrary, among the Sarswatas of the Punjab, what were merely hypergamous groups formerly, now threaten to be separate castes, and when this transformation becomes complete, it will be quite as impossible to count their sub-divisions as those of the Guzratis.

PART III.
THE BRAHMANS OF NORTHERN INDIA.

CHAP. I.—THE BRAHMANS OF BENGAL.

EXCEPTING the recent immigrants from other provinces, the Brahmans of Bengal proper are divided into the following classes :—

1. Paschatya Vaidikas (Lit. Vedic Brahmans of Western India).
2. Radhiyas (Lit. Brahmans of Râdh or Western Bengal).
3. Barendras (Lit. Brahmans of Bârendra country, the name given to the northern part of Bengal).
4. Dâkshinatya Vaidikas (Lit. Vedic Brahmans of Southern India).
5. Madhya Sreni (Lit. Brahmans of the midland country *i.e.*, of the district of Midnapore which forms the border land between Orissa and Bengal Proper).

It is said that there is, besides these, another class in Bengal called the Sapta Satis, or the Seven Hundred, who were the only Brahmans in Bengal before the colonisation of the five priests invited by King Adisur in the 9th century of the Christian era. I have never met with any Sapta Sati Brahmans; but, so far as my information goes, members of this class may be found in some parts of East Bengal, and especially in Maheshpore in the eastern part of the Nadiya district. They usually intermarry with the Râdhiyas, and, for all practical purposes, may be regarded as a section of that class.

§ 1.— *The Pāschātya Vaidikas.*

The numerical strength of the Pāschātya Vaidikas is not very considerable. Their name indicates that they came from the west, and according to the traditions in their families, they are of the Kanojia stock, their ancestors having, at the commencement of Mahomedan rule, migrated from their original habitat to Tirhoot, and subsequently from Tirhoot to Bengal. Most of the Vaidika immigrants were specially invited by one or other of the many Hindu Rajas, who ruled over the country as semi-independent chiefs, during almost the entire period of Moslem ascendancy. The ancestor of the leading Vaidikas of Nadiya was a reader of the *Mahābhārat* who could recite it from memory, and was made to settle in Bengal by a Raja Kāshinath, who was the ruler of the Nadiya district before it was given by the Emperor Jehangir to Bhava Nanda, the ancestor of the present Raja of Nadiya. The founder of the Vaidika family of Kotālipāhār was invited from Kanoj by a Hindu prince who ruled over the district of Bākergunge in the thirteenth century, and was led to celebrate at an immense cost a religious ceremony for avoiding an evil that was foreboded by the fall of a dead vulture on the roof of his palace. The lucky priest secured for himself, by way of remuneration for his services, a valuable zemindari which is now in the possession of his descendants. The most important colonies of the Vaidikas are to be found now in the districts of Nadiya, Burdwan, 24-Pergunnahs, Malda, Rajshahi, Jessore, Bākergunge, Dacca and Faridpore.

The majority of the other classes of Bengali Brahmans are the spiritual disciples of the Vaidikas of Nadiya and Bhātpārā. A Vaidika never enlists himself as a disciple of a Brahman of any other class. Some Vaidikas have Sudra disciples, and have even stooped so far as to officiate as priests for Sudras and in public temples. But, generally speaking, their Brahmanical pride is such that the poorest among them would rather die than do any kind of manual work. Till recently they kept themselves aloof from English education and Government service. But their disciples do not submit nowa-days to be taxed by them to the same extent as in former times, and stern necessity has been compelling the Gurus of Nadiya and Bhātpārā to pocket their pride, and to qualify themselves for Government service and the liberal professions, by English education.

The usual surname of the Vaidikas is Bhattacharya. There are some in the class who have other family names such as Chackravarti, Roy and Chowdry ; but all these are honorific titles, and are not peculiar to the class. For the meanings of these titles, see Glossary.

§ 2.—*The Rārhiya Brahmans of Bengal.*

The Rārhiya and the Bārendra Brahmans of Bengal trace their descent from the five priests brought from Kanoj, in the 9th century, by King Adisur of East Bengal, for the purpose evidently of performing one of those Vedic sacrifices for which competent priests could be had only in the capitals of the great Hindu kings. The Rārhiyas and Bārendras are very proud of their descent. But even on the supposition that King Adisur was a Ksatriya, and not a Vaidya, it cannot be said that, according to Hindu notions, the five priests imported by him were entitled to be regarded as very high class Brahmans. The very title of Upādhya, which their patron gave them, shows that they were regarded as middle class, and not first class, Pandits. The Rārhiyas and the Bārendras may, with much better reason, boast of having had in their clans such great men as Raghunnāth, Gadādhar, Kulluka and Raghunandan, the last being by way of pre-eminence known throughout India as Smarta Bhattacharya, or the great professor of jurisprudence and theology.

The Rarhis derive their clan name from that of the tract of country which now forms the northern portion of the Burdwan division. Brahmans of this class are to be found in every part of Bengal proper, and their numerical strength is perhaps greater than that of all the other classes of Bengali Brahmans taken together. They are divided into about one hundred sub-classes, and grouped under the four main heads mentioned below:—

1. Kulin (families of high lineage).
2. Bansaja.
3. Sudha Srotriya (pure Vedic scholars).
4. Kashta Srotriya (impure Vedic scholars.)

A Rārhiya Kulin can give his daughter only to a Kulin. If he gives his daughter to a Bansaja or Srotriya his Kulinism is destroyed forever. A Kulin can marry the daughter of a Kulin or that of a Sudha Srotriya. If he marry the daughter of a Kashta Srotriya, he is lowered at once in rank. If he marry into a Bansaja family, his Kulinism lasts for some generations in a decaying condition, and his descendant in the eighth degree becomes a regular Bansaj. A Kulin who first marries into a Bansaj family generally gets a very high premium. The Kulins who have kept their Kulinism intact, generally find great difficulty in marrying their daughters, and are obliged to keep them unmarried, notwithstanding the Shastric injunctions that require every Hindu to give his female children in marriage before puberty. A Srotriya can give his daughter to a Bansaj as well as to a Kulin. A Bansaj cannot give his daughter to a Srotriya.

The usual and peculiar titles of the Rārhiyas are:—

1. Mukhopādhya.
2. Bandyopādhya.
3. Chattopādhya.
4. Gangopādhya.
5. Ghosāl.

Each of the first four of these titles consists of two words joined together. The first word is the name of the village* granted to the ancestor of the holder by

---

* This is in accordance with the explanation of the above-mentioned names given by Rārhiya Gattaks or College of Heralds. But Banodh being the ancient name of the tract of country, including the modern districts of Unao and Rai Bareilly in the vicinity of Kanoj, it is quite possible that Bandyopādhya means an Upādhaya of Banodh. Similar explanations seem to be possible regarding Mukhopādhya, Chattāpādhya and Gangopādhya.

King Ballalal Sen, and the last word is Upádhya, which means an assistant teacher or priest. The Rádhis have also other titles such as Putitunda, Kanji Lal, Pakrasi, &c., which are peculiar to their class; but an exhaustive enumeration of these is unnecessary in a book like this. Among the Rádhiyas, there are also Bhattacharyas, Majumdars, Roys, Chowdries, &c., but these titles are not peculiar to their class.

Formerly the Rádhiyas of the eastern and central districts of Bengal devoted themselves generally to the cultivation of Sanskrit, and abstained from all such pursuits as are considered to be derogatory to the dignity of a Brahman. But even under the Mahomedan rulers some of them accepted service as, for instance, Bhabananda Majumdar of Nadiya, and the unfortunate Raja Nand Kumár who, according to Macaulay himself, " had been great and powerful before the British Empire in India began to exist, and to whom in the old times Governors and Members of Council, then mere commercial factors, had paid court for protection."*

---

* Macaulay describes Nand Kumár as a "Brahman of Brahmans," and, at the same time, as the blackest monster in human form. Whether morally he was a worse or a better man than the Judge who convicted him "in order to gratify the Governor-General," or the Governor-General who, according to Macaulay's own showing, was the real prosecutor, is a question which does not fall within the scope of this work. But it may be mentioned here that Nand Kumár was not a high caste Brahman, and was very far from being the head of the Brahman community as Macaulay has represented him to have been for artistic colouring of the picture. Nand Kumár was in fact a middle class Rádhiya Brahman, whose family had once been outcasted, and regained their status partly by a humiliating and expensive ceremony of expiation, and partly by forming connections with families of a higher status. The inaccuracy in the description of his caste status given by a foreign historian is pardonable, but it is impossible to give him credit for impartiality. Apart from the trumpery charges on which Nand Kumár was convicted of felony, the head and front of his offending was that he had intrigued against Hastings for thwarting his ambition to be the Deputy of the East India Company in the place of Mahomed Reza Khan. The Nabob of Moorshedabad had recommended him for the office, and the Court of Directors, in a manner, ordered that he should be appointed to it. But Hastings "bore no goodwill to Nand Kumár. Many years before they had known each other at Moorshedabad, and then a quarrel had arisen which all the authority of their superiors could

Under British rule the Rādhiyas, and especially their outcasted Pirāli section, have been the first to adapt themselves to the exigencies of the new *régime*, and to take advantage of such opportunities for advancement as it offered to the people of the country. Dwarka Nath Tagore and Prasanna Kumar Tagore were Pirālis. Ram Mohan Roy and Ishwar Chandra Vidyāsagar were Brahmans of a better class, but even they did not hold a very high position in their caste. In fact until recently

---

hardly compose." Such being the attitude of Hastings towards Nand Kumār, it is no wonder that he carried out the orders of the Court of Directors only so far that he dismissed Mahomed Reza Khan, and removed the exchequer from Moorshedabad to Calcutta. But the office of Naib Dewan was abolished, and Nand Kumār was subjected to a cruel disappointment. So "it was natural," according to Macaulay himself, "that the Governor should from that time be an object of the most intense hatred to the Brahman." When the Councillors appointed by the Regulating Act arrived, and, possibly in accordance with instructions from the Ministers of the Crown, tried to upset the power of Hastings and indirectly that of the East India Company, Nand Kumār by a natural process became associated with the enemies of the Governor-General. Hastings had mortally offended Nand Kumār. When the latter saw his opportunity he tried to have his enemy disgraced. The enemy retaliated by having the Brahman *murdered* under colour of legal proceedings.

According to Brahmanical ideas of morality Nand Kumār deserves to be condemned in the strongest terms possible for the vices of office-seeking and vindictiveness which he betrayed. But the impartial historian cannot condemn him without condemning also in severer terms the conduct of a man in the position of Hastings, who retaliated insult by murder. If the rules of political morality be different from those of ordinary morality, and if the exigencies of the situation in which Hastings was placed justified the "sharp antidote" that he used, surely the conduct of Nand Kumār towards him ought to be judged by the same standard. But while the great English historian showers every kind of vituperation not only on Nand Kumār, but on the nation itself to which he belonged, he exculpates Hastings with an amiability that is not often found in the old parents of a spoilt only son. After observing that it is impossible to speak too severely of Impey's conduct, the great historian goes on to add :—

"But we look on the conduct of Hastings in a somewhat different light. He was struggling for fortune, honour, liberty, all that makes life valuable. He was beset by rancorous and unprincipled enemies. From his colleagues he could expect no justice. He cannot be blamed for wishing to crush his accusers."

Certainly the defence embodied in the above applies quite as much to Nand Kumār as to Hastings, yet, according to the verdict of the great English historian, Hastings was a politician to whom the ordinary rules of morality do not apply, while Nand Kumār and the nation to which he belonged are villains.

the high class Rādhiyas were usually quite illiterate. Their hereditary rank made them highly prized as bridegrooms for the daughters of their well-to-do clansmen, and many of them lived in former times by making marriage their sole profession. A Kulin of a high class might then marry more than a hundred wives without any difficulty, and there are still some who have such large numbers of wives as to necessitate their keeping regular registers for refreshing their memory, about the names and residences of their spouses. Not only each marriage, but each visit by a Kulin to his wife brought him valuable presents, and as his wives and children were supported by his fathers-in-law, he could pass his days in comfort without being qualified for any kind of service or profession. The Kulin's sons sometimes became rich by inheriting the property of their maternal relatives. But it was until lately very rare for a Kulin to be the architect of his own fortune. The state of things in Hindu society is, however, undergoing great changes. Most of the Kulins have become lowered in rank by marrying into inferior families, and Kulinism, even where it is preserved intact, is not now-a-days valued in the matrimonial market to the same extent that it used to be in former times. Wealth, university degrees and official position command a much higher premium at present than an ancient pedigree. The Kulins themselves have been taught, by the bitter experience of their ancestors, to be not too eager for polygamy. And the *coup de grace* to the practice has been given by a decision of the Bengal High Court declaring that, according to the law of the Shastras applicable to all Hindus, even the Kulins are bound to give maintenance to their wives. Whatever be the cause, monogamy is now becoming the rule among the Kulins, and they are fast on the way towards again taking their proper place among the most refined and cultured classes of the country. A Kulin of the highest rank has just retired on pension after having served the Government of Bengal for several years as Head Assistant in the Judicial Department. Even among the greatest of the living celebrities of Bengal there are at present some Kulins of a more or less high position in the Rādhiya peerage, the foremost among them being Mr. W. C. Bonnerjee, Advocate, Bengal High Court ; Dr. Guru Das Banerjee, Judge, Bengal High Court ; Mr. Pramada Charan Banerjee, Judge, N.-W. P. High Court; Mr. Pratul Chandra Chatterji, Judge, Panjab Chief Court.

The late Mr. Justice Anookul Chandra Mookerji was also a Rādhiya Kulin. Mr. W. C. Bonnerjee is a member of the clan called *Pandit Ratni* or "the jewel of Pandits," and is lineally descended on his mother's side from the great Jagannāth, the author of the Digest translated by Mr. Colebrooke. Babu Pratul Chandra is of the Kharda clan. His grandfather made a fortune by marrying the daughter of Gokool Ghosal, one of the chief fiscal officers in the early days of the East India Company, and the founder of the Raj family of Bhu Kailas.

§ 3.—*Bārendras.*

The Bārendras trace their origin from the same stock as the Rādhis, *i.e.*, from the five priests invited by King Adisur from Kanoj. The Bārendras derive their class name from the ancient name of North Bengal. Their numerical strength is less than that of the Rādhis, but greater than that of the Vaidikas.

The usual family names of the Bārendras are the following :—

1. Lāhiri.
2. Bhādari.
3. Sānyal.
4. Maitra.
5. Bagchi.

These surnames are peculiar to the Bārendras. They have also among them Bhattacharyas, Majumdars, Joadars, Roys, and Chowdries. There are some high caste Bārendras who have the Mahomedan title of Khan. The Bārendras, like the Vaidikas, never do any kind of menial work, and the only class of Bengali Brahmanas who serve as cooks are the Rarhis of West Burdwan. The Rarhis of the eastern districts of Bengal, *i.e.*, of the districts to the east of the river Hooghly, are quite as aristocratic as the Bārendras and the Vaidikas.

The hypergamous divisions among the Bārendras are similar to those of the Rarhis in certain respects, the only important difference being that the Bārendras have a section among them called Cāp* who have a somewhat unique position, though resembling to some extent the Bansaj among the Rarhis.

Polygamy is rare among the Bārendras; but the marriage of a daughter among their higher classes is quite as expensive as among the Rarhis. There are many big Bārendra landholders, the most noted among

---

* With regard to the origin of the Cāps it is said that they are the descendants of a great Kulin named Madhu Moitra by his first wife. Madhu was an inhabitant of a village on the river Atrai, situated near the place where it is now crossed by the North Bengal State Railway. An inferior member of the clan, being treated at a dinner party of his castemen with great contumely, determined to form a matrimonial alliance with the great Kulin at any cost, and with that object hired a boat to take him to the vicinity of Madhu's residence and was careful to have with him on board of the vessel his wife, an unmarried daughter and a cow. On reaching the neighbourhood of Madhu's village, he inquired of a Brahman, who was saying his prayers after performing his ablutions on the banks of the river, whether he knew where the great head of the Bārendra clan lived. The Brahman, who was interrogated, was himself the person about whom the enquiry was addressed. When the fact was made known to the Brahman on board the boat, 'he produced a hammer and a chisel threatening to sink the boat with all its inmates unless Madhu agreed to marry the Brahman's daughter. The old man was too far advanced in life to be quite ready for complying with any request of the kind. But, as an orthodox Hindu, he could not take upon himself any share of the three great crimes, namely, the killing of a female, the killing of a Brahman, and the killing of a cow—which were threatened to be perpetrated in his presence. So he reluctantly gave his consent. But when his sons came to know what he was going to do they were very much annoyed, and they separated from their father at once. The old man was supported by his sister's husband, who was then the other great Kulin of the caste, and the sons who separated became Cāps. The position of their descendants is superior to that of the Srotriyas, but inferior to that of the Kulins. Matrimonial alliance between a Kulin and a Cāp reduces the former to the position of the latter.

them being the great house of Nattore that held possession of more than one-third of Bengal proper, at the time of the conquest of the country by the East India Company. Next in importance to the Nattore Rajas, but more ancient than their family, is that of the Putia zemindars. The late Maharani Sharat Sundari, whose name is venerated throughout India for her extensive charities, and for her character as a model Hindu widow, was a member of the Putia house. Among the other great Bārendra landholders of Bengal are the zemindars of Susang and Muktagacha in the district of Mymensing. Babu Mohini Mohan Roy, who is one of the most successful pleaders of the Bengal High Court, and who has lately been made an Additional Member of the Supreme Legislative Council of India, is a Bārendra.

The majority of the Vaidikas, Rarhis and Bārendras are moderate Saktas. They worship all the ancient deities of the Hindu pantheon; but Durgā, Kāli and Siva have the largest share of their devotion. Many of them sacrifice goats and buffaloes before the deities they worship; but among such of their orthodox members as are not affected by English education, and the temptations of modern town life, the drinking of spirituous liquors is still practically unknown.

§ 4.—*The Dākshinatya Vaidikas.*

The name of this class indicates that they originally came from the south. They are found chiefly in the district of Midnapore, and seem to have been originally Brahmans of Orissa. A few small colonies of the Dākshinatyas are to be found in the southern portion of the metropolitan district of 24-Pergunnahs. They are a separate caste altogether, and there can be neither intermarriage nor interchange of hospitality between them and the Pāschātya Vaidikas. Pandit Siva Nath Sastri, of the Sadharan Brahmo Samaj, is a Dākshinatya Vaidika.

§ 5.—*The Madhya Sreni Brahmans of the district of Midnapore.*

The Madhya Srenis are a very backward class of Brahmans, to be found only in the district of Midnapore. As they have the very same surnames and Gotras as the Rādhis of Bengal, they are evidently a section of the Rādhis. They themselves profess to be so, and account for their want of connection with the Rādhis properly so-called, by saying that as they refused to acknowledge the authority of the Ghataks to determine their status, the Rādhi College of Heralds refused to recognise their very existence. The true cause of their forming a separate caste seems, however, to be that they accepted the gifts of the Kaibartas, and lived in an out-of-the-way district. The Madhya Srenis are generally very poor and without any literary culture beyond what is necessary for doing the work of a priest.

The distinction between Kulins and Srotriyas is not recognised by the Madhya Srenis. The descendants of those who, at one time or other, became famous as Sanskrit scholars, enjoyed, until lately, a higher position than the secular Brahmans. But at present, the status of a party for matrimonial purposes depends chiefly upon the amount of wealth possessed by him. The Madhya Srenis partake of the hospitality of the Kaibartas, and minister to them as priests in all ceremonies except Shradhs.* The Shradhs of the Kaibartas are performed by a class of Brahmans called Vyasokta.

---

* Mr. Risley in his account of the Madhya Srenis says that they have eight Gotras, and that the Madhya Srenis of Mayna and certain other places have a higher position than the rest. But his account seems to be based upon erroneous information.

CHAP. II.—THE BRAHMANS OF MITHILA AND BEHAR.

§ 1.—*Maithilas*.

The Brahmans of Mithila or Tirhoot are called Maithila Brahmans. They form one of the five leading classses of North Indian Brahmans called Panch Gaur. They have no sub-castes, though they are divided into many groups which are of importance for the purpose of arranging marriages among them. The following are the names of these hypergamous groups:—

1. Srotriya or Sote (Lit. A reader of the Vedas).
2. Jog (A family of an inferior class that has attained a superior status by marriage connections with Srotriyas).
3. Panji Badh (Recognized by the local College of Heralds).
4. Nagar.
5. Jaiwar.

A man of a higher group may take in marriage a girl from a lower group. But a girl of a higher group is never given to a bridegroom of a lower class, except where the parents of the former are too poor to marry her to a boy of the same or a superior group.

The Maithila Brahmans have a special kind of headdress. Their usual surnames are the following:—

1. Misra (A reader of the two Mimansas).
   Ojha or Jha* (Both are corrupted forms of the Sanskrit word Upādhya, which means an assistant teacher or priest).
3. Thākoor (God.)
4. Pāthak (A reader of the Mahābhārat and the Purāns).
5. Pura.
6. Padri.
7. Chowdry.
8. Roy.

---

* Persons who profess to exorcise evil spirits or cure snake-bites are usually called Ojhas, or, by a further corruption of the word, 'Roja.' They do not belong to any particular caste, and are generally low class men.

The Maithilas are very conservative, and still think that it is beneath their dignity to accept service under the British Government, though such feeling has died out completely even among the highest classes of Bengali Brahmans.

The head of the Maithila Brahmans is the Maharaja of Darbhanga. The founder of the family, Mahesh Thākoor, bore a Brahmanical surname. But whether on account of the degradation of that highly honorific title, or on account of their belonging to a royal family, his descendants at present use the Ksatriya surname of Sing. The transformation is exactly the opposite of what has taken place in many Ksatriya families, though the ambition of a Rajput to be elevated from the rank of a Sing (lion) to that of Thākoor (god) is certainly more intelligible, than the desire on the part of any royal family to be degraded from the rank of a god to that of a lion.

Besides the Maharaja of Darbhanga, there are many other families of big landholders among the Maithila Brahmans. One of the most conspicuous of these is the Raja of Banaili, who is the owner of the extensive estate of Kharakpore in the district of Monghyr, but is about to be ruined by family quarrels, mismanagement and litigation. The Purnea Zemindars of Srinagar, who are also big landholders, are a branch of the Banaili family. The Banaili family belong to that division which is called Jog.

From very early times Mithila has been famous for the cultivation of Sanskrit. It has given birth to some of the greatest authorities in Hindu jurisprudence, and in the branch of Hindu philosophy called Nya. The great lawgiver Yajnavalkya is described in the opening lines of his work as a native of Mithila, and tradition still points to a place near the junction of the Ghogra with the Ganges, which is believed to have been the residence of the sage Gautama, the founder of the Nya philosophy. Of the mediæval and modern

Maithila authors, the names of Gangesha Upādhya, Pakshadhar Misra, Udayanacharya, Chandeshwar and Bachaspati Misra will continue to be honoured so long as Hindu law and philosophy remain in existence. Among the Maithila Sanskritists of recent times, the late Pandit Bapu Jan Jha attained great eminence, and his son, Chumba Jha, is fully sustaining the reputation of the family. The other two great living Pandits of Mithila are Halli Jha and Vishwa Nath Jha.

The majority of the Maithila Brahmans are Sakti worshippers. They offer sacrifices before the deities they worship, and eat flesh and fish, but are not known to be in the habit of drinking spirituous liquors, as the extreme Saktas are required to do by their Shastras. The Maithila Brahmans do not smoke tobacco.

§ 2.—*Sakaldipi Brahmans of South Behar.*

There is a class of Brahmans in South Behar who call themselves Sakaldipis or Sakadipis. The majority of them live either by ministering to the other castes as priests, or by the practice of medicine. There are, however, a few Pandits and landholders among them. One peculiar custom in the community is that, like the Sarswat Brahmans of the Panjab, a Sakaldipi may marry within his Gotra, though such marriage is strictly prohibited among the three superior castes by Hindu law. The Sakaldipis are divided into a certain number of Purs or sections, and marriage is impossible only within the Pur.

CHAP. III.—THE BRAHMANS OF THE NORTH-WESTERN PROVINCES AND OUDH.

The most important classes of Brahmans in the North-Western Provinces and Oudh are the following :—

1. Kanojia. | 2. Sarujuparis. | 3. Sanadhya.

Kanojia.—The Kanojias hold a very high position among the Brahmans of Northern India. They form one of the five divisions called Panch Gaur, and the Brahmans of Bengal take a great pride in claiming to have been originally Kanojias. The name is derived from the ancient Hindu city of Kanoj, at the confluence of the Ganges and the Kalinadi, in the district of Farrakkabad. The Kanojia Brahmans are to be found in almost every part of Northern India. But their original home is the tract of country which, before the time of Wellesley, formed the western half of the kingdom of Oudh, including the modern districts of Philibit, Bareilly, Shajehanpore Farakkabad, Cawnpore, Fatehapur, Hamirpur, Banda and Allahabad. The usual surnames of the Kanojia Brahmans are the following :—

1. Awasti.
2. Misra.
3. Dikshit.
4. Sukul.
5. Dobey or Dwivedi.
6. Tewari or Trivedi.
7. Chaube or Chaturvedi.
8. Pande.
9. Bajpai.
10. Pati

In each of these there are many sub-sections, having different positions for matrimonial purposes.

The Kanojias, notwithstanding their high position from the point of view of caste, freely enlist in the army as sepoys, and do not consider it beneath their dignity to serve even as orderlies, peons and gate-keepers. The title Pānde has a very bad odour with Englishmen since the Mutiny of 1857. But as a class the Kanojia Brahmans are very remarkable for their aristocratic demeanour and manners, and for their quiet and inoffensive nature. They seldom give way to bad temper, and the practice of any kind of cruelty seems to be quite inconsistent with their general character. They acted no doubt like fiends in some of the episodes of the sepoy revolt. But "the greased cartridge" was a matter serious enough to lead any Hindu to the perpetration of things far worse. Would the British soldiers willingly obey their officers if ordered to bite the dead bodies of their enemies in a battle field? And if they disobeyed the order, and in doing so subjected their officers to any kind of insult or ill-treatment, would any reasonable man find fault with them? The whole world would be horrified at any coercive measure for enforcing such a perverse order. The situation of the sepoys with respect to the "greased cartridge" was exactly the same, and yet it is thought that they have not sufficiently expiated by either being hanged in batches from the boughs of trees, or by being blown away from guns.

There are learned Sanskritists as well as good English scholars among the Kanojias. Many of them practise agriculture, and it is said some till the soil with their own hands. The majority of them are Sivites. There are among them a few Saktas and Srivaishnavas also. The Sivites and Srivaishnavas are strict vegetarians. There are some ganja-smokers and bhang-eaters among the Kanojias, but very few that would even touch any kind of spirituous liquor.

The late Pandit Sheodin, who was prime minister of Jaipore for several years, was a Kanojia Brahman of Moradabad.

Sarujuparia.—The Sarujuparias derive their name from the river Saruju which flows past the city of Ayodhya. They are most numerous in the vicinity of the river Ghogra. They are said to be a branch of the Kanojias. But whatever may have been their original connection there can be no marriage at present between the two classes, and they must be held to be independent castes. The usual family names of the Sarujeeans are the same as those of the Kanojians. There are good Sanskritists among the Surorias. They never till the soil with their own hands.

Sanadhya.—The Sanadhyas are also said to be a branch of the Kanojia tribe. They are very numerous in the central districts of the Doab, between Mathura to the south-west and Kanoj on the north-east. They live chiefly, as shopkeepers and pedlars. The number of educated men among them is very small. The following are their usual surnames :—

1. Misr.
2. Pānde.
3. Dube or Dwivedi.
4. Tewari or Trivedi.
5. Choube or Chatervedi.
6. Upādhya or Ojha.
7. Pāthak.
8. Boidya.
9. Dikshit.
10. Parasar.
11. Devalya.
12. Goswami.
13. Katori.
14. Khenoriya.
15. Tripoti.
16. Choturdhuri or Chowdry.
17. Samadiya.
18. Monas.
19. Bratahari.
20. Chainpuria.
21. Bhotiya.
22. Modaya.
23. Sandaya.
24. Udenya.
25. Chushondiya.
26. Barsya.

The late Guru of the Maharaja of Jaipore, who was believed to have the power of working miracles, and who was venerated as a saint by most of the great Hindu potentates of Central India and Rajputana, was a Sanadhya.

CHAP. IV—THE BRAHMANS OF THE KURUKSHETRA COUNTRY.

Gaur Brahmans.—The original home of the Gaur Brahmans is the Kurukshetra country. The Gaurs say that the other four main divisions of North Indian Brahmans were originally Gaurs, and have acquired their present designations of Sarswat, Kanya-kubja, Maithila and Utkal by immigrating to the provinces where they are now domiciled. The name Adi Gaur adopted by the Kurukshetra Brahmans is in consonance with this view. In Sir George Campbell's *Ethnology of India*, it is suggested that the Gaurs may have derived their name from the river Ghagar, which, in ancient times, was a tributary of the Sarswati, and which now discharges its water into the Sutlej near Ferozepore. According to popular usage the word Gaur means a priest, and it is not impossible that the name of Gaur Brahmans was given to those who served as priests to the ancient kings of Kurukshetra. The Adi Gaurs practise agriculture and till the soil with their own hands. But there are many good Sanskritists* among them, and they are the only Brahmans whom the Agarwala Baniyas would employ as their priests. There is a class of Gaur Brahmans called the Taga Gaur. These

---

* One of the greatest of these is Pandit Laksman Sastri, of Patiala, now residing in Calcutta, from whom I have derived the greater part of the information contained in this chapter. The late Pandit Gauraswami, who was the first Pandit in his time in the holy city of Benares, was also a Gaur.

are so designated because they have only the Brahmanical Taga or sacred thread. They are all addicted to agriculture, and are quite ignorant of the Brahmanical prayers and religious rites. They neither study the Shastras nor perform the work of a priest. The other castes do not make to them the kind of humble salutation (*pranam*) due to Brahmans, but accost them as they would a Rajput or Baniya by simply saying " *Ram Ram.*" Some of the Adi Gaurs are now receiving English education. The general surname of the Gaurs is Misra. Their special surnames are the following :—

1. Dikshit.	9. Mota.	17. Gandharwal.	25. Nagarwal.
2. Tiwari.	10. Indouria.	18. Randyana.	26. Sathya.
3. Chaube.	11. Haritwal.	19. Pantya.	27. Vajare.
4. Nirmal.	12. Bhanchaki.	20. Jhundiya.	28. Simaaant.
5. Nagwan.	13. Mrichya.	21. Kanodiya.	29. Durgawal.
6. Ohahanwal.	14. Ghagaun.	22. Gautama.	30. Khernal.
7. Marhota.	15. Vidhata.	23. Gugwal.	31. Surahya.
8. Lata.	16. Phoratwal.	24. Mudhalwan.	

The majority of the Gaurs are Sivites. Like the other high caste Brahmans of Northern India they worship also the Salagram ammonite as an emblem of Vishnu, and a triangular piece of Phallic stone representing the Devi or the consort of Siva. There are a few Ballabhachari Vaishnavas among the Gaurs. The majority of the Gaurs are strict abstainers from animal food and intoxicating drinks. Some of the Gaurs keep the sacred fire, and occasionally celebrate some of the Vedic sacrifices.

CHAP. V.—THE BRAHMANS OF KASHMIR, THE PANJAB AND SINDH.

§ 1.—*Bramhans of Kashmir.*

Kashmiri Brahmans. — The usual surnames of the Kashmir Brahmans is Pandit. The following observations in Sir George Campbell's *Ethnology of India* give an exact description of their ethnology and character :—

> The Kashmiri Brahmans are quite High Aryan in the type of their features, very fair and handsome, with high chiselled features, and no trace of intermixture of the blood of any lower race * * * * The Kashmiri Pandits are known all over Northern India as a very clever and energetic race of office-seekers. As a body they excel the same number of any other race with whom they come in contact.—*Ethnology of India,* pp. 57-59.

The late Mr. Justice Sambhu Nath Pandit of the Bengal High Court was a member of this class. So was also the late Pandit Ayodhya Nath, who was one of the ablest advocates of the Allahabad High Court, and also one of the principal leaders of the Congress. Babu Gobind Prasad Pandit, who was one of the pioneers of the coal mining industry of Bengal, was also a Kashmiri. He amassed such wealth by the success of his enterprise, that he became known as one of the richest men in the country in his lifetime, and, after his death, his descendants obtained the title of Maharaja from the Government of India.

Dogra Brahmans.—As there are Dogra Rajputs and Dogra Baniyas, so there is a class of Brahmans. called

Dogra Brahmans. The name is said to be derived from that of a mountain or valley in Kashmir. According to a Dogra student of Nya philosophy at Nadiya, whom I consulted, the name is derived from the Sanskrit compound Dwan Gartau, which means the "two valleys."

§ 2.—*The Brahmans of the Panjab.*

Sarswats.—The Brahmans of the Panjab are chiefly of this class. They derive their name from that of the sacred river Sarswati, which at a very remote period of antiquity was a noble river, and the course of which may still be traced from its source near the sanitarium of Simla to Thaneshur in the Kurukshetra. The Sarswats form one of the five primary classes of North Indian Brahmans, called Panch Gaur. A great many of the Sarswats practise agriculture, and freely partake of the hospitality of the Baniyas and the Kshetris. There are, however, many among them who are very erudite Sanskritists* and who, in point of culture and Brahmanical purity, are not inferior to the Brahmans of any other class. The majority of the Sarswats are Sakti worshippers, but very few of them eat flesh. They minister to the Kshetris of the Panjab as priests, and there is, in many respects, a close connection between the two castes. Until recently the Sarswats were divided into only two sub-castes, namely, the Banjais† and the Mohyals. The Banjais

---

* One of the greatest of these is Pandit Sadanand Misra of Calcutta, from whom I have derived a considerable part of the information contained in this chapter. In respect of personal appearance, obliging nature, and refined manners, it is hard to find a superior specimen of humanity.

† The word Banjai seems to be a corrupted form of the Sanskrit compound *Bahu Yaji*, which means a Brahman who ministers to many men. But the Sarswats say that their common name Banjai is a corrupted form of *Bayanna Jayi*, which means the fifty-two victorious clans, and to account for the origin of this name they add that they obtained this name by setting at defiance an order of an Emperor of Delhi directing them to allow the re-marriage of a widow.

minister to the Kshetris, but the Mohyals never serve as priests. There are many hypergamous groups among the Banjais, which are on the way towards becoming separate castes. So long as the lower of these classes gave their daughters in marriage to the higher, they could not be regarded as independent castes. But, in very recent times, the lower classes have resolved not to give their daughters to the higher classes, unless they choose to reciprocate the compliment. The result is that marriage alliances between the different classes are now extremely rare, and they are fast on the way towards becoming independent castes. The general surname of a Sarswat is Misr. But each clan has a special surname. The names of the several hypergamous groups among the Banjai Sarswats together with the special surnames of each class are given below:—

Names of Groups.	Titles.	Names of Groups.	Titles.
1. Panjajati Adrai Ghar and Char Ghar	1. Morlhe. 2. Tekha. 3. Jhingan. 4. Jeteli. 5. Kumoria.	4. Barhi	1. Kaliya. 2. Prabhakar. 3. Lakhan Pal. 4. Airi. 5. Nabh. 6. Chitrachot. 7. Narad. 8. Sarad. 9. Jalpatra. 10. Bhamvi. 11. Paranoty. 12. Manar.
2. Inferior Panjajati	1. Kaliya. 2. Maliya. 3. Kupuria. 4. Madhuria. 5. Bagge.		
3. Ashta Bans	1. Pathak. 2. Sori. 3. Tiwari. 4. Tasraj. 5. Jotashi. 6. Shand. 7. Kurla. 8. Bharadwaj.	5. Inferior Banjais not coming within the above groups	1. Basude. 2. Bijora. 3. Raude. 4. Mehra. 5. Muslol. 6. Sudan. 7. Sutrak. 8. Teri. 9. Angul. 10. Haster.

A Sarswat cannot marry within his clan. But a marriage may take place among them within the Gotra, though such matrimony is strictly prohibited by the Shastras.

The Mohyals are found chiefly in the western districts of the Panjab and in Kabul. Intermarriage between them and the other Sarswats is possible, but not very usual.

§ 3.—*The Brahmans of Sindh.*

The Brahmans of Sindh are mainly Sarswats. They are divided there into the following classes :—

1. Srikara.
2. Bari (Twelve families).
3. Bavanjahi (Fifty-two families).
4. Shetapalas.
5. Kuvachandas.

All these classes eat animal food, though some of them are Vaishnavas of the Vallabhachari sect. Like the Sarswats of the Panjab proper, those of Sindh also eat cooked food from the hands of Kshetris and Roda Baniyas. The Bavanajahis are Sakti worshippers of the extreme class, and not only eat flesh but drink wine. Some of the Shetapalas are also Sakti worshippers of the same type.

In speaking of the several classes of Sindh Brahmans Dr. Wilson says :—

All these classes of Sarswats are Sukla Yajur Vedis. In using animal food they abstain from that of the cow and tame fowls, but eat sheep, goats, deer, wild birds of most species, and fish killed for them by others They also eat onions and other vegetables forbidden in the Smritis. They are generally inattentive to sectarian marks. They dress like the Hindu merchants and Amins of Sindh, though using white turbans. They shave the crown of their heads, but have two tufts of hair above their ears. They are the priests of the mercantile Lohanas or Lowanas. They have many small pagodas dedicated to the worship of the ocean, or rather the river Indus. Their fees are derived principally from their services at the marriages, births and deaths of their followers. They are partial to popular astrology, as far as easy prognostication is concerned. They pretend to know where lost articles are to be found. They also cultivate land, and sometimes act as petty shopkeepers.—Wilson's *Hindu Castes,* Vol. II, pp. 137-138.

CHAP. VI.—THE BRAHMANS OF ASSAM.

THE majority of the Brahmans of Assam profess to be Vaidakas, though, in fact, they practise either the Tāntric or the Vishnuvite cult. The inferior families among them appear to be of the Mongolian race, while even among their most aristocratic classes there appears to have been a copious admixture of Mongolian with Aryan blood. In Upper Assam, including the districts of Sibsāgar and Lakhimpur, which, before its annexation to British India, was for several centuries under the rule of the Ahang dynasty of Sibsāgar, a great many of the Brahman families profess to be descended from seven Kanojia priests imported into the country about the middle of the seventeenth century by the Ahang King Chutumala *alias* Jayadhwaja. The Aryan features of most of the members of these families, and the genealogies preserved by them, give very strong support to their claim; but, at the same time, it is equally certain that there has been a large infusion of non-Aryan blood among them. The fact is conclusively proved by their ethnology, and also by their traditions and customs. They themselves entertain the suspicion that many of the families with whom they now intermarry were originally Sudras, and were made Brahmans only by the edicts of their former kings. That their suspicions are not groundless is proved almost conclusively by some of the curious customs which still prevail among them as to interdining. In other parts of the country, the most puritanic Brahmans do not hesitate to partake of the hospitality of their fathers-in-law or maternal uncles. But among the aristocratic Brahmans of Upper Assam claiming to be descended from the Kanojian stock, no one will eat any kind of food in the house of either his father-in-law or his maternal uncle. It is said that even the daughter of a low class Brahman will not, after being married to a Kanojia of pure descent, eat in her father's house any *kachi* food though cooked by her own mother. The daughter's sons will eat in their maternal grandfather's house till their initiation with the sacred thread, but not afterwards. It seems that in practice, the alleged custom, so far as the daughter and the daughter's sons are concerned, is more honoured in the breach than in the observance. But the very recognition of such rules, if only for theoretical purposes, and the existence of Mongolian and Aryan types in the same families, clearly establish that the higher Brahmans are of the Aryan stock, and that they intermarried with local Brahmans of the Mongolian race, though with a very considerable degree of reluctance.

CHAP. VII.—THE BRAHMANS OF ORISSA.

AMONG the superior Brahmans of Orissa there are two main divisions which rest on territorial bases, and which are as follows:—

1. Dākshinatya or Southern clan.
2. Jajpuria or Northern clan.

There can be no intermarriage between these two divisions, and they have nothing in common between them except the status of being Brahmans.

§ 1.—*The Dākshinatya Brahmans of Cuttack and Puri.*

The Dākshinatya Brahmans of Southern Orissa are subdivided as follows:—

1. Vaidikas or Brahmans devoted to ecclesiastical pursuits which are not held degrading according to the Shastras.
   1. Kulins or Vaidikas of the highest class, who are mostly residents of one of the sixteen Shasan or of the thirty-two Kotbarvillages.

      Surnames.
      1. Samanta.
      2. Misra.
      3. Nanda.
      4. Pati.
      5. Kar.
      6. Acharya.
      7. Satapati.
      8. Bedi.
      9. Senapati.
      10. Parnagrahi.
      11. Nishank.
      12. Bainipati.

   2. Srotriyas or ordinary Vaidikas.
      1. Bhatta Misra.
      2. Upadhya.
      3. Misra.
      4. Rauth.
      5. Ota.
      6. Tewari.
      7. Das.
      8. Pati.
      9. Satapasti.

2. Pujari, Adhikari or Vaishnava Brahmans. Forming one caste, found in every part of Orissa. Same titles as the above.

3. Secular Brahmans divided into two classes designated as follows:—
   1. Mahajanpanthi or Panigri.
   2. Masthan.

   1. Mahapatra.
   2. Panda.
   3. Shaubth.
   4. Senapati.
   5. Nekab.
   6. Mekab.
   7. Pathi.
   8. Panni.
   9. Shathera.
   10. Pashupaloke.
   11. Baru.
   12. Mudhirath.
   13. Doytha.
   14. Poryari.
   15. Khuntes.
   16. Gora Baru.
   17. Nabaka.

The sub-classes that have the highest status among the Dākshinatya Brahmans of Orissa are the Kulins and Srotriyars of the sixteen Shashan and the thirty-two Kotbar villages. The Shashanis evidently derive their name from the fact of their obtaining, from some ancient Hindu king of the country, grants of land attested by Shashanas or royal firmans. The name Kotbar seems to be a corruption of Krobar and to be the proper designation of the suburban population of the Shasanas. The Shashan villages are inhabited only by the Kulin and Srotriya Brahmans of the ecclesiastic class. In the Kotbars there are other castes also.

The Shashani Kulins have a higher status than all the other classes of Orissa Brahmanas. There are a few good Pandits among the Shashanis, and the majority of them acquire a sufficient knowledge of Sanskrit to be able to discharge the duties of a priest. The following observations are made with regard to the class in Hunter's *Gazetteer of India* :—

> They live on lands granted by former Rajas, or by teaching private students, or as spiritual guides, or more rarely as temple priests. They are few in number, for the most part in tolerable circumstances, though often poor, but held in such high estimation that a Srotriya Brahman will give a large dower in order to get his daughter married to one of them. But the Kulin who thus intermarries with a Srotriya loses somewhat of his position among his own people. The pure Brahman rarely stoops below the Srotriya, the class immediately next to him, for a wife.—*The Imperial Gazetteer of India*, Vol. X, p. 434.

The majority of the Srotriyas earn their living in the very same manner as the Kulins. All the Vaidikas are very aristocratic according to Brahmanical ideas of respectability, and a Shashani Kulin or a Srotriya Brahman will rather live by begging than be engaged in any menial occupation. In fact, there are among them, and especially among the landless Srotriyas, a great many who are regular beggars. But it would be hard to find any one of them tilling the soil, or employed as a domestic servant.

The Adhikari Brahmans are mainly followers of Chaitanya, and have the same position in Orissa that the Gossami and the Adhikari Brahmans have in Bengal. It is said that many of the Oriya Pujaris were originally men of low castes. They have generally many low caste disciples, and are employed as priests in the temples. The Adhikari Brahmans are known by the necklace of basil beads which they wear in addition to their sacred thread. They are not all the followers of one teacher, and the disciples of each individual Guru form a distinct subdivision.

Of the several classes of secular Brahmans the Mahajan Panthis or Panigiris have a high position; but the Masthans are regarded as a low class, and their very touch is regarded by some as contaminating.

With regard to the Masthan Brahmans, Mr. Stirling in his *Description of Orissa Proper* says:—

There is another class known commonly in Orissa by the name of Mahasthan or Masthan Brahmans, who form a very considerable and important class of the rural population. Besides cultivating with their own hands gardens of the Kachu (*Arum Indicum*) cocoanut and areca, and the piper betel or pan, they very frequently follow the plough, from which circumstance they are called Halia Brahmans, and they are found everywhere in great numbers in the situation of Mukadams and Sarbarakars, or hereditary renters of villages. Those who handle the plough glory in their occupation, and affect to despise the Bed or Veda Brahmans who live upon alms. Though held in no estimation whatever by the pious Hindu, they are unquestionably the most enterprising, intelligent, and industrious of all the Company's ryots or renters of malguzari land in Orissa. *Asiatic Researches*, Vol. XV., p. 199.

The Pandas who serve as priests and cooks in the public temples receive in their official capacity some homage from other people. But irrespective of their connection with the holy shrines, they are regarded as a very low class everywhere; and throughout the greater part of India they form separate castes with a very inferior status. In Calcutta there are many Panda

Brahmans of Orissa who serve as cooks in the houses of the rich Sudras. The Pandas who tout* for pilgrims are not all of the Panda caste.

§ 2.—*Jajpuria Brahmans.*

Jajpur is one of the sixteen Shasana towns of Orissa, but, as intermarriage cannot take place between the Jajpuria Shasanis, and the Brahmans of the Shashans in Southern Orissa, the Jajpurias form a distinct class, They are said to be divided into thirteen Houses with the following six Gotras :—

1. Kaphala.
2. Kumara.
3. Kausika.
4. Krishnatriya.
5. Kamakayan.
6. Katyaana.

Their usual surnames are Pati, Panda, Das, Misra, Nondkar, Satapati, &c. There are Adhikari and Mahajanpanthi Brahmans in the northern parts of Orissa as in its southern parts. These do not form separate castes, but intermarriage can take place between them, and the corresponding sections of the Brahmanical caste of southern Orissa. The Jajpuria Adhikari are to be found in large numbers in Calcutta, a great many of them being keepers of stalls on the banks of the

---

* The tours of these Oriya touts are so organised that during their campaigning season, which commences in November and is finished by the approach of the car festival at the beginning of the rainy season, very few villages in any of the adjoining provinces of India can escape their visit and taxation. The very appearance of one of them causes a serious disturbance in the even tenor of every Hindu household in the neighbourhood. Those who have already visited the "Lord of the World" at Puri are called upon to pay an instalment towards the debt contracted by them while at the sacred shrine, and which debt, though paid many times over, is never completely satisfied. That is, however, a small matter compared with the misery and distraction caused by the "Jagannath mania," which is excited by the Pandas' preachings and pictures. A fresh batch of old ladies become determined to visit the shrine, and neither the wailings and protestations of the children, nor the prospect of a long and toilsome journey can dissuade them. The arrangements of the family are, for the time being, upset altogether, and the grief of those left behind is heightened by the fact that they look upon the pilgrims as persons going to meet almost certain death. The railway about to be constructed between Calcutta and Puri may make a visit to Jaggannath a less serious affair.

holy Bhagirathi, supplying the bathers with oil for anointing their persons before ablution, and materials for painting their foreheads with holy figures and names after bathing. In the town of Jajpur there are some families who have been keeping the sacred fire from generation to generation.

Besides the good Srotriyas and Mahajanpanthis there are in Orissa, as in every other part of the country, some classes of inferior Brahmans who are regarded as more or less degraded. One of these classes is called Atharva Vedi.* There may be intermarriage between the followers of Rik, Sham and Yajus, but not between these and the Atharva Vedis. The other classes of degraded Brahmans will be noticed in their proper place.

---

* Some say that the Atharva Vedis are the same as the Masthanis. But the result of my enquiries tends to establish that there are other Atharva Vedis besides the Masthanis.

CHAP. VIII.—THE BRAHMANS OF RAJPUTANA.

To make the description of the Brahmans of Rajputana intelligible, it is necessary to say something about the geography of the province. Broadly speaking, it is that portion of India which lies between the river Chambal on the east, and the valley of the Indus on the west. The greater part of this vast tract of country is ruled still by semi-independent Rajput chiefs, and hence it is called Rajasthan, Raithana or Rajputana. The number of chiefs whose territories collectively go by these names is not less than twenty, and the only British possession within the circuit is the district of Ajmere-Merwara, which lies in the centre of the province. The country of the "Kings' children" is, however, not endowed with much of nature's gifts. It is divided into two parts by the Aravali hills, which extend from Abu on the south to the historic ridge in the suburbs of Delhi. The western half of Rajputana comprising the territories of Marwar, Jesalmere and Bikanir, consists mainly of sandy deserts utterly unfit for growing any kind of food-grains. Of the eastern half which is more fertile, the southern portion is included within the dominion of Udeypur; the central portion is ruled by the chiefs of Kota, Boondi and Jaipore; while the northern portion is taken up by Dholepore, Bhurtpore and Alwar.

Though, according to its very name, Rajputana is the country of the Rajputs, and though the military Ksatriyas are the ruling caste almost throughout its length and breadth, yet its Brahmanical population is twice as large as that of the fighting clans, and the influence of the sacerdotal caste in the province is exactly as it is in other parts of India. There are in Rajputana large colonies of Sarswat, Gaur, Sanadhya and Kanojia Brahmans whose connection with the members of their respective races in their original homes, has not yet been completely severed. Of the several classes of Brahmans whose proper home is Rajputana, the following are the most important:—

1. Srimali ... A numerous clan found in every part of Rajputana as well as in Gujarat.
2. Mewad ... Found chiefly in Mewad.
3. Pallivala ... Most numerous in Western and Northern Rajputana. Found also in Bombay and Gujarat.
4. Pokarana .. Most numerous in the Northern and Western parts of Rajputana. Found in considerable numbers also in Sindh and Gujarat.
5. Sanchora ... Original home Sanchora in Sirohi.
6. Dahima ... Found chiefly in Marwar and Bundi.
7. Divas ... Found chiefly in Bikanir, Marwar and Nathadwara.
8. Parik ... Found chiefly in Marwar and Bundi.
9. Khandelwal Found chiefly in Marwar and Jaipore.
10. Nandwani Bora. Found chiefly in Marwar and Kesouli.
11. Sikhawal ... Found in Jaipore.
12. Asopa ... Found in Marwar.
13. Rajgor ... Found in every part of Rajputana.
14. Gujar Gor ... In every part of Rajputana.
15. Bhojaks ... Low class Brahmans who minister to the Jains.

The Bhats and the Charanas, who are the hereditary bards and genealogists of Rajputana, claim to have the rank of Brahmans, but as they are not regarded as such by Hindu society, I shall speak of them in the part of this work which is devoted to the semi-Brahmanical castes. I conclude this chapter with a few details of the more important sections of the Rajputana Brahmans, collected chiefly from English authorities.

§ 1.—*The Srimalis.*

The Srimalis have a very high position whether regarded from a religious or secular point of view.

THE SRIMALI BRAHMANS.

They minister as priests not only to the Srimali Banyas, but to all the higher castes including the Brahmans of the other classes. They hold also very high offices in the service of the local chiefs.

The following account of the Srimalis is taken from Wilson's *Indian Castes* :—

The Srimalis derive their designation from the town of Srimal, now called Bhinmal, lying to the north-west of Abu and intermediate between that mountain and the river Lomi. Their first representatives are said to have been collected by a local prince from no fewer than forty-five of the most sacred places of the north, west, south and east of India; but to the traditions to this offcct little importance is to be ascribed. The Aryan physiognomy is perhaps more distinctly marked in them than in any other class of Brahmans in India. In fact, they do not appear to differ much from the type of some of the European nations, especially of those who have claims to Roman descent. Their costume is generally of a simple but not unbecoming character. Their turbans are on the whole of a graceful form, though not so large as those of many of the other natives of India. On their brows they wear the sectarial marks of the Vaishnavas, Vishnu being their favourite doity. The Srimalis are now scattered not only through several of the provinces of Rajputana, but through Gujarat and Kacha, Central India, the countries bordering on the Indus, and the island of Bombay. In consequence of this dispersion of their body, they have been broken into several distinct castes, most of which now neither eat nor intermarry with one another. They are also divided into two castes, founded on the Vedas which they profess : the Yajur Vedi (White and Black), and the Sama Vedi of the Kauthumi Sakha. In the former there are seven gotras or lines of family lineage: the Gautama, Sandilya, the Chandras, Laudravon, Maudralas, Kapinjalas. In the latter there are also seven gotras, the Shaunakas, Bharadvaj, Parasara, Kausika, Vatsa, Aupamanya, and Kashyapa. Most of all their classes are either mendicants or officiating priests, though secular service appears to be on the increase among them. They act as gurus and ceremonial Brahmans to the Srimali, Poraval, and Patolya and Urvala Vanyas (merchants) and Sonis or goldsmiths; and about 5,000 of them, now apart from their brethren, act as gurus to the Oswalas, a class of mercantile Jainas, and are called Oswala Brahmans. A favourite Kuladevi or family goddess among them is that of Mahalaksmi, the spouse of Vishnu, a celebrated image of whom was transferred from Bhimmal to Auhilpur, or Pattan in the times of the Gujarat kings. The celebrated Sanskrit poet Magh, who is said to have lived in the time of Bhoja Raja, belonged to their fraternity. Their greatest living ornament is Dalpatram Daya, the Kaviraj, or Poet Laureate of Gujarat, who is also distinguished for his historical research, and sincere aims at social reform. This stirring author and singer supposes that there are 500 Srimali houses in Kacha and Kattiwar; 5,000 in Gujarat; and 35,000 in Marwad and Mewad, exclusive of 50 of impure birth called *Daskort* near Ahmedabad, 1,500 of them being in Jodhpur (the capital of Marwad) alone.—Wilson's *Indian Castes*, Vol. II, pp. 109—111.

§ 2.—*Pallivals.*

The Pallivals are numerous in Jesalmere, Bikanir, Marwad, Jaipur and Kishangarh. Very few of the clan are to be found in Ajmere. The following account of the Pallival Brahmans of Rajputana is also taken from Dr. Wilson's *Indian Castes* :—

The Pallival Brahmans receive their name from the town of *Palli, the commercial capital of Marwad in Rajputana. They have twelve gotras. They are shrafs, merchants, and cultivators, but serve only in their own caste. They don't eat or intermarry with other Brahmans. They are found in Jodhpur, Bikanir and Jesalmere, and some others of the Rajput States. A few of them are at Delhi, Agra, and in the Panjab, Gujarat and Mewad. Only one or two of them are in Bombay. They are Smartas and do not use animal food. They do not drink the water of the houses of their own daughters † or any persons not belonging to their own castes. They don't eat with those of their own caste, who have got isolated from them as with the Gurjas and Mewad Pallivalas. They belong to the Kanya Kubja division of the Brahmans. "The Nandavana and Pallivala Brahmans are traders; were formerly located at Nandavana and Palli, and were there chiefly robbers, conducting their excursions on horseback. They subsequently became traders. They are said still to worship a bridle on the Dasara in memory of their former state."‡ They are scattered throughout the north of India, as Bohras or middlemen between the cultivators and Government.—Wilson's *Indian Castes*, Vol. II, p. 119.

The following account of the Pallivals of Jesalmere is from Tod's *Annals of Rajasthan* :—

Next to the lordly Rajputs, equalling them in numbers and far surpassing them in wealth, are the Pallivals. They are Brahmans, and denominated Pallivals from having been temporal proprietors of *Palli* and all its lands, long before the Rathores colonized Marwar. Tradition is silent as to the manner in which they became possessed of this domain; but it is connected with the history of the Palli, or pastoral tribes, who from the town of Palli to Pallitana, in Saurashtra, have left traces of their existence; and I am much mistaken if it will not one day be demonstrated that all the ramifications of the races figuratively denominated *Agnicula* were Palli

---

* "PALLI."—Town in Jodhpur State, Rajputana, situated on the route from Nasirabad to Disa, 108 miles to the south-west of the former cantonment. An ancient place acquired by the Rahtors of Kanoj in 1156 A.D. It is the chief mart of Western Rajputana, being placed at the intersection of the great commercial road from Mandavi in Cutch to the Northern States, and from Malwa to Bahalpur and Sind —Hunter's *Imperial Gazetteer*, Vol. XI, p. 1.

† Here Dr. Wilson has evidently misunderstood the information given to him. The custom spoken of here is not the speciality of the Pallivals, but is a common one to all the orthodox Hindus throughout India. It is based not on any aristocratic feeling on the part of the father, but to too much obedience to the injunction of the Shastras forbidding the acceptance of any kind of gift from a son-in-law.

‡ Irving's *Topography of Ajmere.*

in origin: more especially the Chohans, whose princes and chiefs for ages retained the distinctive affix of *Pal.*

These Brahmans, the Pallivals, as appears by the Annals of Marwar, held the domain of Palli when Seoji, at the end of the twelfth century invaded that land from Kanoj, and by an act of treachery first established his power. It is evident, however, that he did not extirpate them, for the cause of their migration to the desert of Jesalmere is attributed to a period of a Mahomedan invasion of Marwar, when a general war contribution (*dind*) being imposed on the inhabitants, the Pallivals pleaded caste and refused. This exasperated the Raja, for as their habits were almost exclusively mercantile, their stake was greater than that of the rest of the community, and he threw their principal men into prison. In order to avenge this they had recourse to a grand *chandi* or act of suicide; but instead of gaining their object, he issued a manifesto of banishment to every Pallival in his dominions. The greater part took refuge in Jesalmere, though many settled in Bikanir, Dhat and the valley of Sind. At one time, their number in Jesalmere was calculated to equal that of the Rajputs. Almost all the internal trade of the country passes through their hands, and it is chiefly with their capital that its merchants trade in foreign parts. They are the *Metayers* of the desert, advancing money to the cultivators, taking the security of the crop; and they buy up all the wool and ghi (clarified butter) which they transport to foreign parts. They also rear and keep flocks. The Pallivals never marry out of their own tribe; and directly contrary to the laws of Manu the bridegroom gives a sum of money to the father of the bride. It will be deemed a curious incident in the history of superstition, that a tribe, Brahman by name, at least, should worship the bridle of a horse. When to this is added the fact that the most ancient coins discovered in these regions bear the Palli character and the effigy of the horse, it aids to prove the Scythic character of the early colonists of these regions, who, although nomadic, wore equestrian. There is little doubt that the Pallival Brahmans are the remains of the priests of the Palli race, who, in their pastoral and commercial pursuits, have lost their spiritual power.—Tod's *Rajasthan,* Vol. II, pp. 318—320.

§ 3.—*The Pokaranas.*

The Pokaranas are very numerous not only in every part of Rajputana, but in Gujarat and Sind also. They derive their designation from the town of Pokarana, which lies midway between Jodhpore and Jesalmere. The priests at Pushkar are called Pushkar Sevakas or the "worshippers of the lake." The Pokarana Brahmans have no connection whatever with the holy lake called Pushkara near Ajmere. They are devoted chiefly to secular pursuits. They are also the priests of the Bhatyas, and there are a few among them who are good Sanskritists and astrologers. They do not eat any kind of animal food. Their physiognomy is distinctively Aryan.

CHAP. IX.—THE BRAHMANS OF CENTRAL INDIA.

By Central India is meant the part of Northern India enclosed by the river Chambal on the west, the river Narmada on the south, the upper half of the Sone on the east, and the valley of the Jumna on the north. The majority of the Brahmans settled in this tract are foreign immigrants belonging chiefly to the Maharashtrya, Gujrati and Kanojia stocks. The only classes of Brahmans whose original home can be said to be Central India are the following :—

1. Malavis ... Found chiefly in Malwa.
2. Narmadis ... Found chiefly on the banks of the Narmada.
3. Jijhotia ... Found chiefly in and near Bundelkhand.

The Jijhotias derive their designation from the old name* of Bundelkhand. As there are Jijhotia Brahmans so there are Jijhotia Banyas and Rajputs also. The usual surnames of the Jijhotia Brahmans are the same as those of the Kanojias. It deserves to be noted here that among the Jijhotia Brahmans there is a Mauna Gotra apparently derived from the name of the great Hindu legislator.

---

* The name of Jijhota is mentioned in Huen Tsiang's *Travels*.

PART IV.
THE BRAHMANS OF SOUTHERN INDIA.

CHAP. I.—PRELIMINARY REMARKS.

It has been already observed that both according to the Shastras and the popular belief of the people of this country, the Brahmans of India are divided into ten classes, of which five are natives of Northern India, and the remaining five have their habitat in the Deccan. The majority of the Deccani or Panch Dravira Brahmans are Sivites. The number of Vishnuvites among them is also very considerable. But there are very few Sakti worshippers among them, and they are strict abstainers from every kind of animal food and intoxicating drink. The Sivites paint three horizontal lines of white colour on their forehead. The Vishnuvites have perpendicular lines of red, black or yellow colour painted on their foreheads between the upper part of the nose and the scalp. The colour and the form of the lines differ in the different sects, of which a full description is given in a subsequent part of this work. Some of the Vishnuvites of the Deccan are regularly branded like cattle, either only once when they are first initiated in the privilege of the mantra, or from time to time whenever they are visited by their spiritual preceptors. Among the South Indian Brahmans the line of demarcation between the ecclesiastics and the laity is maintained with much greater strictness than in Northern India. In Bengal and Hindustan proper, a Brahman devoted to secular pursuits is not deemed to be altogether incapable of performing the functions of a Guru or priest, or of receiving religious gifts. For the discharge of clerical functions, those who do not stoop to any kind of secular employment are generally deemed to be best qualified. But in the North religious donations are very often given to, and received by, the secular Brahmans, and cases are known in Bengal in which the privilege of even administering the mantra has been allowed to be exercised by graduates of the Calcutta University, and by persons in the service of Government. The case, however, in Southern India is different. There the laity cannot accept religious gifts, and are debarred altogether from the performance of clerical work. Throughout the greater part of the Deccan, a Bhikshu may at any time become a member of the secular order, and intermarriages take place usually between the ecclesiastics and the laity. But in the Andhra country the distinction is carried to a far greater extent than anywhere else. There the laity form a different caste called Niyogis, and there cannot possibly be any intermarriage between them and the Vaidikas. Throughout the Deccan the laity are called *Laukika* Brahmans; and the ecclesiastics have the designation of *Bhikshus*. Another peculiar feature, common to the several classes of South Indian Brahmans, is the fact of their being all subject to the spiritual authority of the Sankarite monasteries. This fact has been noticed already. *See* p. 16, *ante*.

CHAP. II.—THE BRAHMANS OF GUJARAT.

Though Gujarat is situated to the north of the river Narmada, yet, according to Shastric texts, the Gujarat Brahmans form one of the main divisions of the Panch Dravira or the sacerdotal class of Southern India. The majority of them are either Sivites or Vishnuites. But it is said that there are a few Saktas among them of an extreme type not to be found in Bengal. The profession of the Guru is said to be unknown among them. It may be so among the followers of the ancient Sivite cult, the actual nature of which is by very few clearly understood or thought of. But, considering the character of the rites said to be practised by the Gujarati Saktas and Vaishnavas, it does not seem likely that the Guru is less active among them than in other parts of the country.

Every Gujarati's name consists of two parts: the first part being his own name, and the second that of his father. The usual surnames of the Gujarati Brahmans are Bhatta, Yani, Sukkul, Upādhya and Vyas.

The number of separate clans among the Gujarati Brahmans is very large. They generally say that there are not less than 84 different sections among them. The list given in Wilson's *Hindu Castes* includes 160 independent clans among them. However that may be, the following are the most important:—

1. Audichya
2. Nagar
3. Raikwar
4. Bhargava
5. Srimalis
6. Girnar

These are the most aristocratic clans among the Gujarati Brahmans. There are very few among them who live by begging or manual work. But a great many of them have a high secular position, and the majority of them are in well-to-do circumstances. Of the other clans, the Sanchoras usually serve as cooks. The Valodras are, generally speaking, very well-to-do people, a great many of them being money-lenders on a large scale. But they all go about the country begging for alms. They usually perform their tours on horseback.

§ 1.—*Audichyas.*

The Audichyas, as their name indicates, profess to have come from the north. According to their traditions and the *Audichya Prakas*, a reputed section of the Skanda Purana, their origin is stated to be as follows :—

> Mulraj, King of Anhilwara Pattana, the Hindu capital of Gujarat, collected the following numbers of Brahmans from the different sacred places mentioned :—From the junction of the Ganga and Yamuna 105; from the Chyavanasrama 100; Samavedis, from the country of Kanya Kubja 200; from Kashi 100; from Kuru Kshetra 272; from Gangadvara 100; from Naimisha forest and from Kuru Kshetra, an additional supply of 132, making a total of 1,109. He conferred upon them as a Krishnarpan, the town of Sihor, with 150 adjoining villages, and the town of Sidhapura, with 100 adjoining villages. By this liberality he did what satisfied those Brahmans denominated the Sahasra (thousand) Audichyas. But other intelligent Audichyas did not accept his dana (largesses) but forming a *toli* of their own, became the Talakya Audichya, who acquired for themselves Khambhat (Cambay) and twelve other villages; while of the others 500 were of Siddhapara and 500 of Sihor.—Wilson's *Indian Castes*, Vol. II, p. 94.

According to the above account, the Audichyas ought to be divided into the following three classes only :—

    1. Tolakya Audichyas.
    2. Siddhapuria Audichyas.
    3. Sihor Audichyas.

According to the Audichya Brahmans of Gujarat whom I have been able to consult, there are many independent sections among them, of which the following are the most important:—

1. Tolakya.
2. Siddhapuria.
3. Sihoria.
4. Sahasra ...{ 1. Jhalwari. 2. Khariri. 3. Gohelwari. }
5. Kherwar.
6. Unawar.
7. Gharia.

There can be no intermarriage between these sections, and, for all practical purposes, they are separate castes though they may eat together without violating any rule of caste.

Siddhapur is an ancient town and a place of pilgrimage within the territories of the Baroda Raj. Sihor is within the Bhaunagar State, Kathiwar, about 13 miles west of the Bhaunagar town. Its ancient names were Sinhapur and Sarswatpur. It formed the capital of the Gohel Rajputs until Bhaunagar town was founded.

The Jhallwaris take their name from the district of Jhallwar in Kathiwar. Kherali is a petty State in the Jhallwar division of Kathiwar. Gohelwar is a tract of country to the south-east of Kathiwar, and forms one of its four main divisions. Kheral is a petty State in Mahi Kantha, a province of Gujarat. Una was an ancient town in Junagarh State, ruled at one time by the Unawar Brahmans. Its modern name is Dalawar. Garh is the name of a petty State in Rewah Kanth, Gujarat.

The majority of the Audichyas are devoted to secular pursuits. But there are many among them who are regular beggars. There are a few Vedic Pandits in the class. But the number of these is not very considerable. Wilson says that some of the Audichyas act as domestic servants in the capacity of water carriers. Considering how proud the Brahmans usually are, that may seem as quite impossible. But the existence of the practice among the Gujrati Brahmans is borne out by the result of my own enquiries. The Siddhapurias like, many other classes of Brahmans, may be found to be engaged as cooks; and the Siddhapuria cooks are said to be very expert in their line.

§ 2.—*Nagar Brahmans of Gujarat.*

The Nagar Brahmans are the priests of the Nagar Banyas. There are very few Sanskrit scholars among them. But they count among their numbers many who hold and have held high secular positions. The main divisions among them are the following:—

1. Vadnagara.
2. Vishalnagora.
3. Sathodra.
4. Prasnora.
5. Kishnora.
6. Chitroda.

The information which I have been able to collect regarding these several classes of the Nagara Brahmans coincides in all material points with what is given about them in Wilson's book. I therefore cite from it *in extenso* the following account of them:—

The *Vadnagora Brahmans* receive their designation from the city of *Vadnagora* lying to the east of Aunhilavada Pattana. They are mostly found in the Peninsula of Gujarat, formerly Saurashtra, now Kathiwar, where the business of the native estates is principally in their hands; but individuals of them are scattered over nearly the whole of the province of Gujarat, being found at Nadiyad, Ahmedabad, Baroda, Surat, &c. Most of them are Rig-Vedis, following the Sankhyana Sutras; but some of them profess the other three Vedas, particularly the White Yajur Veda. The majority of them are Smartas; but an inconsiderable number of them are Vaishnavas of the sects of Swami Narain and Vallabhacharya. None of them are practical cultivators, but a few of them act as Desais. The mendicants among them are few in number. They do not eat even with the Nagars of other denomination's.

The Vishalnagora Brahmans receive their name from the town of Vishal, founded by Vishal, the first king of the Vaghela dynasty of Gujarat, sometimes called Visaldeva (said by Colonel Tod to have been installed in Sumvat 1249, A.D. 1192) and which lies a little to the south-west of Vadanagora. They are principally Rig-Vedis, and are either Smartas or Vaishnavas of the sect of Swami Narain. They are mainly either public servants or agriculturists.

The Sathodra Brahmans get their name from the town of Sathod on the Narmada. There are some Rig-Vedis among them; but they are principally of the Madhyandina Sakha of the White Yajur Veda. They are found at Anand, Nadiyad, Ahmedabad, Dabboi and other places. Some of them are in public service, or engaged in buying and selling; but a good many of them are still Bhikshus, or act as *Gurus*. They are principally if not wholly Smartas.

The Prasnoras are said to belong to Prasnora. They are Rig-Vedis, and of the Vallabhacharya sect, their chief residence being in Kathiwar. They are principally mendicants.

The Krishnoras of Krishnapura are of the Rig, Sama, and Yajur Vedas. Most of them are Bhikshukas of a "kind respectable for learning."

The Chitrodas are of the town of Chitrod. They are found at Bhaunagar and Baroda. They say that they have among themselves professors of each of the Vedas. They are not a numerous body.

The present Dewan of Baroda, Mr. Muni Bhai, is a Vadnagora Brahman. So was also Mr. Gouri Shankar, Udaya Shankar, c.s.i., formerly Dewan of Bhaunagar, whose portrait is given in Sir Monier Williams's recent work on *Brahmanism and Hinduism.*

§ 3.—*The Raikwar Brahmans of Gujarat.*

The Raikwars are to be found chiefly in Kach and in the district of Kheda in Gujarat. There are many Sanskritists and English scholars among them. The spiritual guide of the Rao of Kach is a Raikwar; so is the eminent Pandit Badri Nath Trimbak Nath. Mr. Bhai Sankar, who is one of the leading attorneys of the Bombay High Court, is also a Raikwar.

§ 4.—*The Bhargava Brahmans.*

The chief habitat of the Bhargavas is the district of Broach at the mouth of the Narmada. The name of the tract inhabited by them is evidently a corrupted form of the Sanskrit Bhrigu Kshettra, the territory of Bhrigu. The Bhargavas were formerly one of the poorest and most ignorant of all the classes of Gujarati Brahmans. In Wilson's book it is stated that, under the British Government, they were certainly rising. The correctness of his forecast is demonstrated by the fact that there are now many learned men and high officials among them.

§ 5.—*The Srimalis.*

The Srimalis are, properly speaking, Brahmans of Rajputana, and an account of them has been given in the chapter on Rajputana Brahmans in Part III, Chapter VIII, p. 66, *ante.*

Mr. Dalpatram Daya, C.I.E., the celebrated poet of Gujarat, and the author of the work on caste entitled "Gnati Nibandha," is a Srimali of Ahmedabad. The great Sanskrit poet *Māgha* is also said to have been a Srimali.

The Srimali Brahmans of Gujarat have the following sub-divisions among them :—

1. Kachi Srimali.
2. Kathiwadi Srimali.
3. Gujarathi Srimali.
4. Ahmedabadi Srimali.
5. Surati Srimali.
6. Khambhati Srimali.

§ 6.—*Girnars.*

Wilson gives the following account of the Girnar Brahmans :—

The Girnars derive their name from the ancient mountain city of *Girinagar,* now represented by Junagadh, the old fort at the root of the celebrated Girnara mountain. In this locality they are principally to be found. They are also met with in other towns of the peninsula of Gujarat. A few of them are in Bombay. They are divided into the following castes.
(1) The *Junagadhya Girnaras.*
(2) The *Chorvada Girnars* of the town of Chorvad on the coast of the peninsula of Gujarat between Pattana Somnath and Mangrol.
(3) The *Ajakyas,* so called from the village of *Ajak.*
These three castes readily eat together, but do not intermarry. They now rank low in the Brahmanhood, from their acting as *Gurus* to Kolis, and having a variety of occupations as those of administrators to native chiefs, clerks, astrologers, cultivators and mendicants. They are of various sects as suits them for the time being. They are said to profess all the Vedas but the Sama, but are principally of the White Yajur Veda. They must be a very ancient confederation of Brahmans.—Wilson, Vol. II, p. 101.

§ 7.—*The other Classes of Gujarati Brahmans.*

The other classes of Gujarati Brahmans are mentioned in the following list with brief descriptive notices :—

1. *Anavalas or Bhatelas.*—Found chiefly in the tract of country between Broach and Daman. The Bhatelas are secular Brahmans, the majority of them being devoted to agriculture and trade. Some of them are employed as Government servants and mercantile assistants.

2. *The Borasidhas.*—These derive their name from the town of Borsad in the Kaira district, Bombay Presidency.

3. *The Chovishas.*—This tribe has representatives at Baroda, and at Sinor and Janor near the Narmada.

4. *The Dadhichis.*—Numerically a small body. Found chiefly on the Mahi. There are beggars, cultivators and ecclesiastics among them.

5. *The Dashaharas.*—Said to be found near Aunilwara Pattan. They are Sakti worshippers.

6. *The Deswali.*—Literally, the people of the country. They are found chiefly in the district of Kheda.

7. *The Jambus.*—The Jambus are the Brahmans of the town of Jambusara in the district of Broach. There are cultivators as well as mendicants and astrologers among them.

8. *The Khadayatas.*—The Khadayatas are chiefly of the ecclesiastical profession, acting both as priests and *Gurus*. They are to be found in the districts of Khedra, Ahmedabad and Broach.

9. *The Masthanas.*—The Masthanas are found in large numbers in the vicinity of Siddhapura. Like the Masthanas of Orissa, those of Gujarat also are chiefly cultivators.

10. *The Modhas.*—The Modha Brahmans are to be found chiefly in the districts of Ahmedabad and Kheda. They are the *Gurus* or spiritual preceptors of the Modha Banyas.

11. *The Nandodras.*—So named from Nandod, the capital of the Rajpipla State, situated about 32 miles east by north from Surat in a bend of the Korjan river. The *Gurus* of the Rajas of Rajpipla and Dharmpore are said to be Nandod Brahmans. There are both mendicants and cultivators among the Nandods.

13. *The Naradikas.*—The Naradikas are to be found chiefly in Cambay and its neighbourhood. They are a small body. There are cultivators as well as mendicants among them.

14. *The Narsiparas.*—The Narsiparas are followers of Vallabhacharya. The priests of the shrine of Krishna at Dakor, in the Thasra sub-division of the Kaira district, are Brahmans of this class.

15. *The Parasaryas.*—The Parasaryas are said to be found in the south-east of Kathiwar.

16. *The Sachora.*—The Sachoras are followers of Vallabhacharya. A great many of them serve as cooks.

17. *The Sajhodras.*—So named from the town of Sajodh near Broach. Like that of the Bhatelas the chief employment of the Sajhods is cultivation.

18. *The Somparas.*—The Somparas are the Brahmans who have charge of the temple of Siva at Somenath. They have a somewhat higher position than is usually assigned in the caste system to the priests of other shrines. The Somparas are all Smartas. After the destruction of the great temple at Semenath by Mahmud Ghazni a new one was erected by Bhima Deva I. This new temple was destroyed by the renegade Hindu, Sultan Muzaffer I. The present temple was erected by Rani Ahalya Bai.

19. *The Sorathiyas.*—The Sorathiyas derive their name from Saurashtra, modern Surat. They are found chiefly in Junagadha.

20. *The Talajyas.*—The Talajyas derive their name from the town of Talaja in the Bhaunagar State, situated about 31 miles south of Bhaunagar town. The Talajyas are now mainly shopkeepers, and are to be found at Jambusar, Surat, Bombay, Nasik and other towns of Western India.

21. *The Tapodhanas.*—The Tapodhanas derive their name from the river Tapti on the banks of which they are to be found. Some of them are priests in the local temples of Siva. But the majority of them are cultivators.

22. *The Valadras.*—The Valadras seem to derive their name from Wala, the capital of the Wala State in

the Gohelwar division of Kathiwar. The ancient name of Wala was Walabhipur. Some of the Valadras are very rich, being money-lenders on a large scale. But the majority of them are mendicants and beggars. Some of the latter class perform their tours on horseback. The Valadras are Smartas and Sakti worshippers.

23. *The Valmikis.*—The Valmikis are to be found in Kheda, Cambay and Idar. There are both beggars and cultivators among them.

24. *The Vayadas.*—The Vayadas are the spiritual preceptors of the Vayada Vanyas. The Vayada Brahmans are a very small body.

The other classes usually included in lists of Guzrati Brahmanas are either foreigners, or degraded and semidegraded Brahmans, corresponding to the Agradānis, Mahā-Brahmanas and Barna Brahmanas of Northern India. The following are like Barna Brahmans :—

1. *Abhira* Brahmans—Brahmans who minister to the Abhira cowherds as priests.
2. *Muchigor*—Brahmans who minister to the Mochis.
3. *Kunbigor*—Brahmans who minister to the Kunbis.
4. *Darjigors*—Brahmans who minister to the darjis or tailors.
5. *Gandharp Gors*—Brahmans who minister to the Gandharps or musicians.
6. *Gurjara Gors*—Brahmans who minister to the Gurjaras.

CHAP. III.—THE BRAHMANS OF MAHARASHTRA AND KANKAN.

THE most important classes of Brahmans in Maharashtra and the Kankan are the following :—

1. Deshastha.
2. Kankanastha.
3. White Yajurvedi.
4. Karhade.
5. Shenavi.

It was on Brahmans of the first four of these classes that the Peshwas bestowed religious gifts, and donations in acknowledgment of literary merit. The last have great secular importance.

§ 1.—*The Deshastha Brahmans of Maharashtra.*

The word *Deshastha* literally means " residents of the country," and, in Maharashtra, the name is given to the Brahmans of the country round Poona, which was the metropolis of the Maharashtra empire. Most of the Deshasthas pursue secular professions as writers, accountants, merchants, &c. However, there were, and still are, among them great Pandits in almost every branch of Sanskrit learning. As among the other classes of South Indian Brahmans, the laity among the Deshasthas are called *Laukikas* (worldly men) or *Grihasthas* (householders). The *Bhikshus* or ecclesiastics are also householders, as every Brahman is required to be in his youth; but as they devote themselves entirely to the study of the Shastras, they alone are held entitled to receive religious donations, and are called *Bhikshus* or beggars. The secular Deshasthas have such secular surnames as Desai, Despande, Desmukha, Kulkarni and Patil. The Bhikshus are sub-divided into several classes, according to the branch of learning which they cultivate. Those who study the Vedas are called Vaidika ; those who expound the law are called Shastri ; those who make astrology their speciality are called Jotishi or Joshi ; the votaries of the medical science are called Vaidyas ; and the reciters of the Purāns are called Purānikas. These distinctions, however, do not affect their caste status. In fact the son of a Laukika Brahman may be a Bhikshu, and a Bhikshu himself may, at any time, by accepting secular employment, cease to be of the ecclesiastical order. The usual surnames of the Bhikshus are Bhatta, Shastri and Joshi.

The Deshasthas are followers of the Rik and the Krishna Yajus. There are some Vishnuvites among them of the Madhwa sect. But the majority are Sivites. There is, however, nothing to prevent intermarriage between the Sivites and the Madhwas. There is a large colony of the Deshasthas in Mysore. There are a great many Brahmans of this class in Benares also. Pandit Govinda Shastri, of the Government Sanskrit College of Calcutta, is a Deshastha. The great Sanskrit jurists, Nilkanta and Kamalakar were Deshasthas. The celebrated Tantia Topi of the Sepoy war was a Brahman of the same class. He was born in a village called Gowala, in the district of Nasik. His proper name was Raghu Nath Rao. Tantia Topi was the name of his boyhood. The late Sir T. Madhava Rao was of the same class.

§ 2.—*The Kankanastha Brahmans.*

As their name indicates, the original home of the Kankanasthas is the Kankan, or the narrow strip of country extending from Broach on the north, to Ratnagiri on the south, and bounded on the west by the Arabian Sea, and on the east by the Western Ghats. The Kankanasthas are also called Chitpavana, a word which evidently means a "purifier or curer of the soul." But on the authority of the Sahyadrikhanda of the Skanda Purāna, which seems to be the composition of a Deshastha, the other classes of Maharatta Brahmans say that Chitpavana is not a corrupted form of Chitta Pāvana, but of Chitāpāvana, which means a purifier of a funeral pyre. According to the Skanda Purāna, the Kankanasthas are so-called because the Brahminical hero and incarnation, Parushuram, created them out of a *chita* or funeral pyre. Leaving aside legends, the name of Chitpavan given to the Kankanastha Brahmans seems to be derived from the town of Chiplun in the Ratnagiri district, situated near the head of the Kumbharli pass, which is one of the easiest routes from the Deccan to the sea-board. The Peshwas, who very nearly succeeded in establishing Hindu supremacy in India during the last century, were Kankanastha Brahmans. Of the same class also were many of the high officials of the Mahratta empire—the Patvardhanas, the Gokales, the Rastyas, &c.

Raja Dinkar Rao, who was Prime Minister of Scindia at the time of the Sepoy war, and who was regarded as one of the greatest administrators of his time, was a Kankanastha. Mr. Justice Ranade, of the Bombay High Court, is a Brahman of the same tribe. So was the late Rao Saheb Vishwanath Narayan Mandalika, who was one of the ablest advocates of the Bombay High Court, and was also a Member of the Legislative Council of India.

As among the Deshasthas, so among the Kankani Brahmans, the majority are devoted to secular pursuits. They are the persons who generally fill "offices of every kind, including the village and perganah accountantships all over the country."* A great many of them are *khotes* or landholders, who enjoy valuable proprietary over the Kankan villages. Though mainly secular, the Kankanasthas do not keep themselves quite aloof

---

* Campbell's *Ethnology of India*, p. 73.

from the cultivation of letters. On the contrary, they have had among them some of the best scholars in every department of learning. One of the greatest of these in recent times was the late Pandit, Bapu Deva Sastri of the Government Sanskrit College, Benares. The following is from the appreciative notice of his life in Mr. Sherring's *Hindu Tribes and Castes* :—

> Bapu Deva Sastri has greatly distinguished himself as a scholar, and has, by his works, shed a lustre on the Sanskrit College, in which for many years he has been a Professor of Mathematics and Astronomy, and on the city in which he lives. The titles of some of his numerous works are as follows : On Trigonometry in Sanskrit ; Translation of the Surya Siddhanta into English ; On Algebra in Hindi ; On Geography in Hindi ; On Arithmetic in Sanskrit ; Symbolical Euclid in Sanskrit.
> In consideration of the great services rendered to science and education in India, the Sastri has been made an Honorary Member of the Royal Asiatic Society of Great Britain, and also of the Asiatic Society of Bengal.—Sherring's *Hindu Tribes and Castes*, Vol. I, p. 90.

Like the Deshasthas, the Kankanis are followers of the Rik and the Krishna Yajus. The Rig Vedis are of the Ashwalayana Sakha, and the Yajur Vedis of the Taittiriya Sakha. The following are sub-classes of the Kankanasthas :—

1. Nirvankor.
2. Keloskar.

The Kankanis have more than three hundred surnames peculiar to their class.

§ 3.—*The Yajurvedis.*

The Yajurvedis among the Desbasthas are followers of the Black Yajus. The class of Maharatta Brahmans called Yajurvedi are followers of the White Yajus. They have two branches, namely,—

1. The Kanvas.
2. The Madhyandinas.

The Kanvas are so called on account of their adopting the Kanva rescension of the White Yajus. The Madhyandinas derive their name in the same manner from the Madhyandina Sakha of the White Yajus. Both the

Kanvas and the Madhyandinas follow the Shatapatha Brahmana, and the Srauta Sutras of Katyana. The Madhyandinas* attach great importance to the performance of the Sandhya prayer at noon, *i.e.*, after 11 A.M. But the Rig Vedis might perform the mid-day prayer even at 7 o'clock in the morning. The Madhyandinas cannot celebrate any Sradh except at noon, whereas the Rig Vedis can perform such a ceremony any time during the day. The Yajurvedis are to be found in every part of the Maharatta country, properly so-called, from Nasik on the north to Kolhapur on the south. They enjoy a very high position among the Brahmans of the country. The majority of them keep themselves aloof from secular pursuits, and devote themselves entirely to the study of the sacred literature and to the practice of the Vedic rites. During the reign of the Peshwas, they had perhaps the largest share of the religious gifts made by the State as well as in those made by private individuals. The families of the Guru of the Maharaja of Kolahpur, and of the titular Pratinidhi of Sattara are Yajurvedis of the Madhyandina Sakha.

§ 4.—*The Karhades.*

The Karhades derive their name from the town of Karhad near the junction of the Krishna and the Koina rivers, about fifteen miles to the south of Sattara. While the Deshasthas are Sivites, and the Yajurvedis are observers of the Vedic rites, the Karhades are the extreme Saktas of the Maharashtra country. In Northern India, Sivites, Saktas, Vishnuvites, and Vedists are to be found within the same class; and a difference of cult, though giving rise to great animosity, has very seldom brought about the formation of subdivisions in any caste. But in the Deccan, which has been

---

* The name of the Madhyandina Sakha of the White Yajus seems to be derived from that of the Madhyandina School of Hindu astronomers according to whom the day is regarded as beginning at noon, and not at sunrise or midnight.

ruled by great Hindu kings down to recent times, the case is naturally otherwise. The Peshwas were Sivite Brahmans, and, during their ascendancy, the Vishnuvites never could flourish in their country. The only cults, besides that of the Sivite, which then found a congenial soil in the country round Poona, were Sakti worship, which is only the counterpart of Saivism, and the Vedic rites which, though rendered obsolete by more effective and less wasteful forms of worship invented in later times, have still a great charm for the Hindu mind. The Sivite, the Sakta and the Vedic forms of worship have flourished side by side in the Maharashtra country, and naturally there was great bitterness between the professors of these forms of faith. Wherever there are two or more competitors for favour from the same quarter, and each tries to rise in the estimation of the common patron, at the expense of his rivals, sectarian hatred and bigotry must necessarily be rampant.

In the Sahyadri Khanda of the Skanda Purāna, which bears evidences of being the production of a Desastha Brahman, the Karhades are charged with the practice of offering human sacrifices, and of even murdering Brahmans to propitiate their deities. The charge being preferred by an infallible authority, the Karhades admit its truth, though with the usual qualification that the practice has been given up by them long since. As a matter of fact, perhaps, the practice never existed on a large scale among any class of Brahmans. The Tāntras recommending human sacrifice are accepted as authorities by the Brahmans of almost all the classes throughout India. Yet, in practice, the only animals that are usually sacrificed by the Sakti worshippers in Northern India are the goat and the sheep, *i.e.*, the animals, the flesh of which the Brahmans eat. The flesh of the buffalo is eaten by some of the low castes, and sometimes buffaloes are sacrificed by the Saktas. But human sacrifice, though recommended by one set of texts, is prohibited by others, and as it must be naturally revolting to every one excepting a few depraved fanatics, and as actual instances of it are extremely rare, if not quite unknown, in modern times, the case was apparently never very different in mediæval or ancient India. In the Mahābhārt, which is undoubtedly a very ancient work, Krishna himself is made to observe* that the slaughter of human beings for sacrificial purposes was unknown in practice. Coming down to historical times there is nothing in the early records of British rule, or in the Mahomedan chronicles to warrant the conclusion that the practice prevailed very extensively during the last seven centuries. The injunctions about it in the Tāntras were, it seems, meant only to excite awe on the minds of the common people, and to enable the priest to make the votaries more ready to offer as a substitute a goat or a sheep than they would otherwise be. The case is only that of an application of the maxim of priestly politics which the Brahmanical clerics formulate by saying that they must ask for a Kashmere shawl in order to get a bathing towel.

Whatever room there may be for comment on the religion of the Karhades, they are equal to the Kankanasthas and the Deshasthas in every other respect. The great Maharatta poet Moropant was a Karhade. So was the late Bala Gangadhar Shastri Jambhekor, who was a professor in the Elphinstone Institution.

The Karhades distinguished themselves sometimes in secular service also. Govinda Pandit, a Karhade Brahman, was sent by the Peshwa as his agent to Saugor, and the Pandit succeeded in taking possession of the district for his master, from Chattra Sal, in 1753. Sheo Ram Bhao was the Sir Soobah or Governor of the province of Jhansi at the time of the conquest of Northern India by the English. His descendants ruled the province as semi-independent kings, till the annexation of the State by Lord Dalhousie. The Karhade dynasty of

---

* See *Mahābhārt*, Sava Parva, Chapter XXII.

Jhansi has been rendered particularly famous by the name of the great Rani whose political genius and ability as a military commander have elicited the admiration of even English historians and generals. There is still a large colony of Karhade Brahmans in Saugor and Damoh who trace their descent from the companions-in-arms of their great clansmen who first conquered the country. There are many Karhades among the officers of the Mysore Raj, the majority of them being connected with its Revenue Survey Department.

§ 5.—*The Shenavi Brahmans of the Kankan.*

The Shenavis are believed to be a branch of the Sarswat Brahmans of the Panjab. They are found chiefly in the Kankan, Goa, and Bombay. There are a few among them who are of the priestly profession. But the majority of them are devoted to secular pursuits in which they are now generally far more successful than perhaps any other class of Brahmans. Like the Sarswatas, the Shenavis are in the habit of eating fish and such flesh as is not prohibited by the Shastras.

The Shenavis are not all of the same religion. There are Sankarites and Madhwa Vishnuvites among them. The late Dr. Bhau Daji, the late Mr. Justice Telang, and the late Pandit Shankar Pandurang were all Shenavis. So is also Mr. Bhandarkar, the present Vice-Chancellor of the Bombay University.

CHAP. IV.—MIDDLE CLASS AND INFERIOR BRAHMANS OF THE MAHARASHTRA.

§ 1.—*Middle Class Secular Brahmans.*

THE following are the middle class Brahmans of the Maharashtra country :—

1. Deva Ruke.
2. Savashe.
3. Kirvantas.

Deva Ruke.—The Deo Rukes are found chiefly in the Kankan. They are generally very poor. They are devoted mainly to agriculture. The Deshasthas will eat with them ; but the Kankanasthas generally refuse to do them that honour.

Savashe.—The Savashes are found chiefly in the Southern Maharatta country. They engage in trade, and are a prosperous class. The name is evidently derived from the Sanskrit word Sahavasi which means an "associate." The origin of the application of this designation to them is explained as follows :—

> In remote times, a certain Brahman came upon a hidden treasure ; but to his amazement, the contents appeared in his eyes to be all live scorpions. Out of curiosity, he hung one of them outside his house. A little while after, a woman of inferior caste, who was passing by the house, noticed it to be gold, and upon her questioning him about it, the Brahman espoused her and, by her means, was able to enjoy the treasure. He gave a feast in honour of his acquisition of wealth. He was subsequently outcasted for his *mésalliance* with the low-caste female, while those who were with him were put under a ban, and thus acquired the nickname.—*Mysore Census Report*, p. 235.

Kirvantas.—The Kirvantas are found chiefly in the Kankan. Many of them are cultivators. But some of them are very rich, and there are good Sanskrit scholars too among them. They are now being recognized as good Brahmanas by the Kankanasthas.

§ 2.—*Yajaka Brahmans.*

The following classes of Maharashtra Brahmans minister to the Sudras as priests, and have consequently a very inferior position :—

1. Palashe.
2. Abhira.

Palashe.—The Palashes are found chiefly in Bombay and its neighbourhood. They act as priests, astrologers and physicians to the Prabhus, Sutars, Bhandaris, Sonars, and other Sudra castes in Bombay. The high caste Maharutta Brahman say that the Palashes are no Brahmans. But as they are accepted as priests by the many Sudra castes mentioned above, they are certainly entitled to be regarded as one of the sacerdotal clans, however low their status may be.

Abhiras.—The Abhiras are found chiefly in Kandeish. They act as priests to the cowherd caste called Abhira.

§ 3.—*Javala Brahmans.*

The Javala Brahmans have a low status on account of their serving as cooks, and their habit of eating fish. They are found chiefly in the Kankan.

§ 4.—*Agricultural Brahmans.*

The following classes of Maharashtra Brahmans are mainly agricultural, and have a very low status :—

1. Kastas—found in Poona and Kandeish.
2. Trigulas—found on the banks of the Krishna.
3. Sopara—found chiefly in Bassin.

§ 5.—*The Degraded and Outcaste Brahmans.*

The following are the classes of Brahmans that in Maharashtra are regarded more or less as outcastes :—

1. The Hoseini.
2. The Kalanki.
3. Kunda Golaka.
4. Randa Golaka.
5. Brahman Jai.

An account of some of these will be given in a subsequent part of this work. See p. 118, *post.*

CHAP. V.—THE BRAHMANS OF KARNATA.

IN English works on the history and the geography of India, the name Karnatic is usually applied to the tract of country on the east coast of the Deccan between Arcot and Madras. But the name of Karnat is properly applicable only to the tract where Kanarese is the prevailing language. It embraces almost the whole of Mysore with the British districts of North Kanara, Dharwar, and Belgaum of the Bombay Presidency. In external appearance, the Karnat Brahmans differ but little from the Deshasthas of Maharashtra.

The following classes are regarded as the indigenous Brahmans of Karnat:—

1. Babburu Kamme } Derive their name from the Kam-
2. Kannada Kamme } me country situated to the east of
3. Ulach Kamme ... } modern Mysore.
4. Haisaniga ...   Very numerous in the Hassan division of Mysore. The great Madhavacharya, it is said, was a member of this caste.
5. Arvatta Vakkalu { Secular Brahmans; followers of Madhava.
6. Hale Karnataka... { Very numerous in Mysore, but have a low caste status.
7. Karnataka.
8. Vaduganadu ... (Lit. from the north).
9. Sirnadu ...
10. Havika ... { From Haiga, the ancient name of North Kanara.
11. Hubu—Found chiefly in North Kanara.

Of these, the first seven classes are found chiefly in Mysore, and the last in North Kanara. The Havikas or Haigas have their principal home in North Kanara and the Shimog division of the Mysore territories. They claim to derive their name from the Sanskrit word Havya, which means "oblation." Their usual occupation is the cultivation of the supari or areca-nut gardens. But there are among them many who are of the priestly order. The Hubus of North Kanara are a degraded class. A great many of them live either by the practice of astrology, or by serving as priests in the public temples. The Hale Karnatikas of Mysore are considered as a still more degraded class. Their very Brahmanhood is not generally admitted, in spite of their having lately secured a Srimukh from the Sringeri monastery recognising them as a class of the sacerdotal caste. Their chief occupations are agriculture and Government service, as Shanbhogs or village accountants. By way of reproach they are called Maraka, which literally means slaughterer or destroyer. The following account is given of them in the *Mysore Gazetteer* :—

"A caste claiming to be Brahmans, but not recognised as such. They worship the Hindu triad, but are chiefly Vishnuvites and wear the trident mark on their foreheads. They are most numerous in the south of the Mysore district, which contains five-sixths of the whole number. The great majority of the remainder are in Hassan district. They call themselves Hale Kannadiga or Hale Karnataka, the name Maraka being considered as one of reproach. They are said to be descendants of some disciples of Sankaracharya, and the following legend is related of the cause of their expulsion from the Brahman caste to which their ancestors belonged—

One day Sankaracharya, wishing to test his disciples, drank some tadi in their presence, and the latter thinking it could be no sin to follow their master's example indulged freely in the same beverage. Soon after, when passing a butcher's shop, Sankaracharya asked for alms; the butcher had nothing but meat to give, which the guru and his disciples ate. According to the Hindu Shastras, red hot iron alone can purify a person who has eaten flesh and drunk tadi. Sankaracharya went to a blacksmith's furnace, and begged from him some red hot iron, which he swallowed and was purified. The disciples were unable to imitate their master in the matter of the red hot iron, and besought him to forgive their presumption in having dared to imitate him in partaking of forbidden food. Sankaracharya refused to give absolution, and cursed them as unfit to associate with the six sects of Brahmans.—*Mysore Gazetteer*, Vol. I, p. 341.

CHAP. VI.—THE BRAHMANS OF DRAVIRA.

DRAVIRA is the name given to the southernmost part of the Indian Peninsula, including the districts of Trichinopoli, Tanjore, Arcot, Tinnevelly, Kambakonam, and Madura. This tract of country being inhabited by the Tamil-speaking tribes is roughly distinguishable from the provinces of Karnat and Andhra towards its north, the prevailing languages of which are respectively Kanarese and Telugu.

The Brahmans of Dravira are divided into two main classes according to their religion. The followers of Sankaracharya are called Smartas, and those of Ramanuja and Madhava are called Vaishnavas. All the Dravira Brahmans are strict vegetarians and teetotalers.

§ 1.—*The Smarta Brahmans.*

The majority of the Smarta Brahmans are Sivites, and there are very few Saktas or Vishnu worshippers among them. They are all followers of Sankaracharya, and regard the Superior of the Sankarite monastery at Sringeri as their spiritual head. Those among the Smartas who devote themselves entirely to Vedic study and to the practice of Vedic rites are called Vaidikas, and those who earn their living by secular pursuits are called Laukikas. The Vaidikas alone are entitled to religious gifts, and the Laukikas cannot lay claim to largesses for pious purposes. But in other respects the distinction is of no importance whatever, as intermarriage is freely allowed between them.

The usual surname of the Smartas is Ayar. The Sanskritists among them use the title of Shastri while the title of Dikshit is similarly used by those in whose family any of the great Vedic sacrifices has ever been celebrated.

The following are the most important classes of Dravira Brahmans of the Smarta order:—

1. Warma.
2. Brihatcharana.
3. Ashta Sahasra.
4. Sanket.

Warma Brahmans.—The Warma Brahmans are very numerous in and near Tanjore. They are divided into the following classes :—

1. Chola Des.
2. Warma Des.
3. Sabayar.
4. Javali.
5. Eanjeay.

These may eat together, but there can be no intermarriage between them. The late Sir Muttuswami Ayar, of the Madras High Court, was a Warma Des Warma of the Tanjore district. Mr. Subramhanya Ayar, who has been appointed to succeed him on the Bench of the Madras High Court, is also a Warma Des Warma. Sir Muttuswami was not only an able Judge, but a great man in every sense of the term. Upon his death, which occurred in January last, the Chief Justice said of him :—

"We are assembled here to express our very great regret at the loss we have sustained by the death of Sir T. Muttuswami Ayar. His death is undoubtedly a loss to the whole country and the Crown. A profound Hindu jurist, a man with very excellent knowledge of English law, with very great strength of mind possessing that most useful quality in a Judge, common sense ; he was undoubtedly a great Judge, very unassuming in manners, he had great strength of mind and independence of character, his judgments were carefully considered, and the decisions he ultimately arrived at were, in a great majority of instances, upheld in the final Court of Appeal. His advice was often asked for by the Judges of the Court, and—I can speak from experience—was always freely given and was most valuable. He was a man who did honour to the great profession of law, an upright Judge who administered justice without distinction of race or creed, a well read scholar and a gentleman in the best and truest acceptation of the word. The High Court by his death has sustained a heavy loss, a loss which undoubtedly it can ill bear."

The Warma Brahmans paint their foreheads in two different ways. Some have transverse lines of sandal or sacred ashes; while others have a perpendicular line of sandal or Gopichandana.*

Brihat Charana.—Among the Dravira Brahmans the Brihat Charanas are next in importance only to the Warmas. The Brihat Charanas paint their forehead with a round mark of Gopichandana in the centre, in addition to transverse lines of white sandal. Sir Sheshadri Ayar, K.C.S.I., the present Dewan of Mysore, is a Brihat Charana. So is also Mr. Sundar Ayar, Advocate, Madras High Court.

Ashta Sahasra.—The Ashta Sahasras are, generally speaking, more handsome than the other classes of Draviri Brahmans. Like the moderate Sakti worshippers of Bengal, the Ashta Sahasras paint between their eyebrows a round mark which is either of white sandal or of a black colouring material formed by powdered charcoal.

Sanket.—The Sankets are Dravidians, but are found also in Mysore. The Mysore Sankets cannot speak pure Tamil. There are two sub-divisions among them, namely, the Kausika Sanketis and the Bettadapara Sanketis. Their religion and their social customs are the same, but there can be no intermarriage between them.

The following remarks are made with reference to the Sanketis by Mr. Narsimmayangar in his report on the last Census of Mysore :—

The Sanketis are proverbially a hardy, intensely conservative, and industrious Brahman community. They are referred to as models for simultaneously securing the twofold object of preserving the study of the Vedas, while securing a worldly competence by cultivating their gardens, and short of actually ploughing the land, they are pre-eminently the only fraction of the Brahman brotherhood, who turn their lands to the best advantage.—*Mysore Census Report*, 1891, p. 236.

---

* A kind of calcareous clay, said to be obtainable only from a tank near Somnath, where the wives of Krishna drowned themselves after his death.

§ 2.—*The Vishnuvite Brahmans of Dravira.*

The Vishnuvite Brahmans of Dravira are followers of Ramanuja. They are divided into two classes, namely, the Vadagala and the Tengala. An account of these sects will be given in a subsequent part of this work.

The late Mr. Rangacharlu, who was Prime Minister of the Mysore Raj, was a Vadagala Vaishnava. Mr. Bhasyam Ayangar and Rai Bahadur Anandacharlu, who are now the leading advocates of the Madras High Court, and have lately been appointed as Members of the Legislative Council of India, are also Vadagala Vaishnavas of the Tamil country.

CHAP. VII.—THE BRAHMANS OF TELINGANA.

TELINGANA is one of the names of that part of the Deccan where Telugu is the prevailing language. In ancient times this tract of country was included in the kingdoms then called Andhra and Kalinga. At the present time Telingana includes the eastern districts of the Nizam's dominions, in addition to the British districts of Ganjam, Vizigapatam, Godavari Krishna, Nellore, North Arcot, Bellary, Cudapa, Karnoul, and Anantpore. The Brahmans of this part of the Deccan are known by the general name of Tailangi Brahmans. They are mainly followers of the Apastamba Sakha of the Yajur Veda. There are also Rig Vedis among them. Nearly a third of them are Vishnuvites of the Ramanuja and Madhava sects, the rest being Smartas. There are very few Sakti worshippers among them even of the moderate type. Like most of the other classes of the Deccani Brahmans, the Tailangis are strict vegetarians and abstainers from spirituous liquors. The orthodox Tailangi does not smoke tobacco.

The Brahmans of Telingana are sub-divided into several distinct sections. On account of difference of cults there are among them the following three main sub-classes:—

1. Smartas. | 2. Sri Vaishnavas. | 3. Madhavas.

The followers of Madhava form a single caste. The Sri Vaishnavas among the Telingana Brahmans form a distinct caste called Andhra Vaishnava. They are not sub-divided as Vadgala and Tengala like their co-religionists of Dravira. The Smartas are sub-divided into two classes, namely, Niyogi and Vaidik. The Niyogis profess to value *Yoga* or religious contemplation more than Vedic sacrifices. In practice the Niyogis devote themselves mainly to secular pursuits, while the Vaidiks constitute the priestly class. The Niyogis are considered to be eligible for priestly service. But they will never either accept a religious gift, or partake of Shradha food. The several divisions and sub-sections among the Tailangi Brahmans are shown in the following table:—

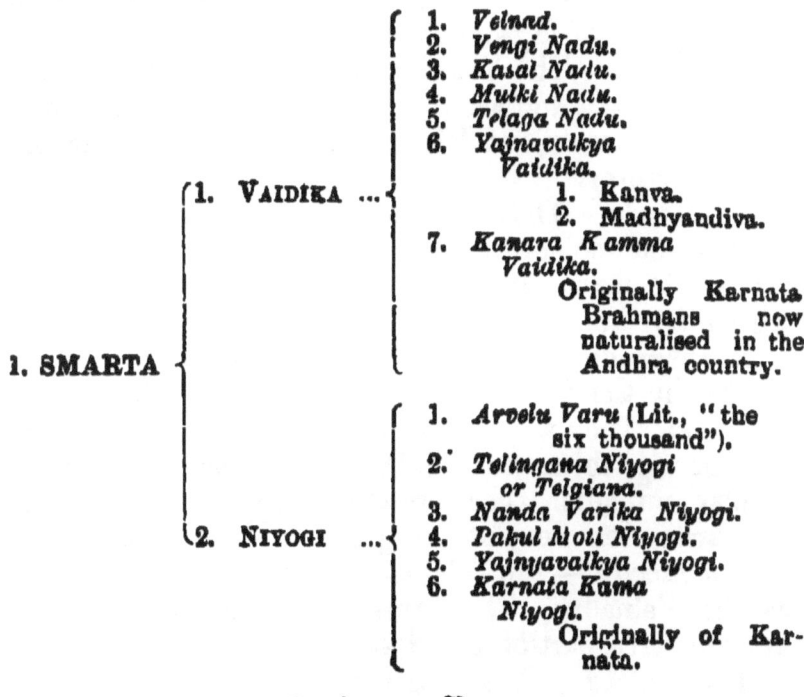

1. SMARTA
  - 1. VAIDIKA
    1. Velnad.
    2. Vengi Nadu.
    3. Kasal Nadu.
    4. Mulki Nadu.
    5. Telaga Nadu.
    6. Yajnavalkya Vaidika.
       1. Kanva.
       2. Madhyandiva.
    7. Kanara Kamma Vaidika. Originally Karnata Brahmans now naturalised in the Andhra country.
  - 2. NIYOGI
    1. Arvelu Varu (Lit., "the six thousand").
    2. Telingana Niyogi or Telgiana.
    3. Nanda Varika Niyogi.
    4. Pakul Moti Niyogi.
    5. Yajnyavalkya Niyogi.
    6. Karnata Kama Niyogi. Originally of Karnata.

2. RAMANUJITES
  1. ANDHRA VAISHNAVAS.
  2. SRI VAISHNAVA—IMMIGRANTS FROM DRAVIRA.
     1. Vadagala.
     2. Tengala.

3. MADHAVA—FOLLOWERS OF MADHAVA.

Velnadu.—The Velnadus are the most numerous class of Tailangi Brahmans. Vallabhachari, who in the 15th century attained great success as a prophet with very little sacrifice of personal ease, and whose descendants are worshipped almost as gods still in Rajputana,

Gujrat and Bombay, was a member of this tribe. According to the Hindustani account of Ballava's "conquests" his father was a native of Kankarkom, but his birth took place at a place named Champa near Raipore, while his parents were on their way from their native village to Benares. A full account of Ballava is given in the part of this book dealing with the Indian sects. The Velnadus are most numerous in the Godavari and Krishna districts. Colonies of the tribe are found also in every part of Mysore except Kadur.

Venginadu.—The Venginadus are next in importance to the Velnadu, and are found chiefly in the British districts of Godavari and Vizigapatam, formerly called the Vengi country.

Kasalnadu.—The Kasalnadus derive their name from Kosala, the ancient name of Oude, from whence they profess to have emigrated to the Kalinga country where they are now found.

Murakanadu.—Brahmans of this class are found chiefly in the tract of country to the south of the Krishna. They are pretty numerous in Mysore. There are among them both priests and men devoted to secular pursuits. The present Superior of the chief Sankarite monastery at Sringeri is a Murakanadu.

Telaganadu.—The Telaganadus are quite as numerous as the Velnadus. The former are found chiefly in the north-eastern part of the Nizam's dominions.

Yajnavalkya.—This name is given in the Telugu country to the followers of the Kanwa Sākha of the White Yajur Veda. They are called also Pratham Sakhi as in the Mahratta country.

Niyogis.—The Niyogis are secular Brahmans. They derive their name from the word *Yoga*, which means religious contemplation, as opposed to *Yaga*, which means religious sacrifice. As the word *Niyoga* in Sanskrit means "employment," it is more probable that the Niyogis are so-called because they accept secular employment. The Komatis and the Sudras bow to them, but the ecclesiastical Brahmans address them with a benediction. From a secular point of view they have great importance. They are usually employed as writers and village accountants.

Aradhyas.—The word Aradhya signifies "deserving to be worshipped." The Aradhyas do not form a separate caste, as intermarriages take place between them and the Smartas. The Aradhyas of the Telugu country profess to be Brahmans, but are, in fact, semi-converted Lingaits, and are not regarded as good Brahmans. Though following Basava in attaching great importance to Linga worship, they adhere to caste and repeat the Gayatri prayers. They act as Gurus or spiritual preceptors to the higher classes of lay Lingaits, while the lower classes among the followers of Basava are left to the guidance of the Jangamas or the priestly Sudras of the sect.

CHAP. VIII.—THE BRAHMANS OF THE CENTRAL PROVINCES.

As a considerable portion of the territories included in what is now called the Central Province was formerly ruled by kings of the Gond tribe, and as there is still a large Gond population in the districts round Nagpore and Jubbulpore, the tract of country inhabited by them is popularly called Gondwana, and the Brahmans settled within it receive the designation of Gond Brahmans. They are called also Jhara Brahmans from the fact of their country being still, to a very large extent, covered by forest. Like some of the Mahratta Brahmans, the Gond Brahmans are divided into distinct sections on account of the differences in the Vedas and the Sákhas which they profess. The majority of them are followers of the Yajur Veda. There are also Rig Vedis among them, but very few followers of any of the other Vedas. The Yajur Vedis are divided into various Sákhas, the Madhyandinas, Kanvas, and the Apastambis being the most numerous. There cannot be intermarriage between these. But marriage alliances are possible between the Rig Vedis and the Apastambi section of the Yajur Vedis. All the Rig Vedis are of the Ashwalayana Sákha.

All the Gond Brahmans are vegetarians and abstainers from intoxicating drink. The Yajur Vedis are chiefly Sivites. There are a few Bhagabats and moderate Saktas among them. The Bhagabats are moderate Vishnuvites, paying reverence to Siva also.

Among the Rig Vedis the majority are Bhagabats and Sivites. There are a few extreme Vishnuvites among them. There may be intermarriage between the Sivites, Bhagabats, Vaishnavas and Saktas of the same class. Intermarriage is possible also between the Bhikshus and the Laukikas.

There are very few wealthy men among the Gond Brahmans. But they have in their community many learned Sanskritists and English scholars. There is in Gondwana a class of Brahmans called Charaki. There are also colonies of the Malwi and the Narmadi.

CHAP. IX.—BRAHMANS OF TULAVA, SOUTH KANARA AND COORG.

Tulava Brahmans.—Tulava is a small tract of country embracing only the British District of South Kanara and a part of Coorg. Udipi, the chief centre of the Madhava sect, is in Tulava, and is regarded by its members as a very holy place.

Dr. Wilson gives the following account of the Tulava Brahmans :—

"The Brahmans taking to themselves the designation of Tulavas are scattered not merely through this province but through some of the territories above the Ghats where they have nearly forgotten their original language. Mr. Stokes mentions the following local varieties of them as found in the Nagara districts :—
  1. Shiwali.
  2. Panchagramadavuru.
  3. Kota.
  4. Kandavaru.

"These are all varieties," he adds, "of Tulava Brahmans, and appear to be almost aboriginal (in a certain sense). They are very numerous in the South of Nagara, Kanladurga, Koppa and Lakavali, where they hold the greatest portion of the betel-nut gardens. They are mostly of Smarta sect, and disciples of the Shringeri and its subordinate Mathas of Tirtha, Muthar, Hariharpura, Bandigadra, Mulavagal, &c. They speak Kanarese only, but their books are partly in the Grantha and partly in the Bal Bodha character. Some sign their names in the Tulava character. They are indifferently educated except a few who are either brokers or in public employ."

The Tulava Brahmans do not intermarry with the other Brahmans on the Malabar Coast. In the regulations, attributed to Sankaracharya, possessed by the Namburi Brahmans, "it is decreed that intermarriages among the Brahmans north of Parampol, forming thirty-two Gramas of Tulanad with the Brahmans of thirty-two Gramas to the south called Malaylam are forbidden.* A synonym of the Tula Brahmans is *Imbran* or rather *Tambaran.*

The Tulava Brahmans resemble the Namburis, and consider themselves as the proper lords of the country, pretending that it was

---
* MS. of Col. Mackenzie, quoted in *South Indian Christ. Repository,* Vol. II, p. 406.

created expressly for their use by Parashurama. They are polygamists. They cohabit, too, Dr. F. Buchanan tells us, with the daughters of the Rajas. Speaking of the Kumali Raja, a professed Ksatriya, he says: "The eldest daughter in the female line cohabits with a Tulava Brahman; her sons become Rajas, and her eldest daughter continues the line of the family. Whenever she pleases, she changes her Brahman."[*] They prevent widow re-marriage, but promote widow prostitution in the name of religion; and with widows and women who have forsaken their husbands and become "Moylar" and attached to the temples, they hold intercourse. They burn their dead. They abstain from animal food and spirituous liquors.

The Tulava Brahmans are equally divided between the sects of Sankaracharya and Madhavacharya.

In Mysore there are some Brahmanic colonists who call themselves Kavarga and Shishyavarga and who are believed to have been originally inhabitants of Tulava. The word Kavarga literally means the first five letters of the Sanskrit alphabet. The reason why the designation is applied to the tribe of Brahmans bearing the name is explained as follows in the report on the last Census of Mysore:—

The name is said to have a reproachful allusion to a legend, according to which a brother and sister of this tribe deceitfully received a gift by representing themselves as husband and wife at a Brahmanical ceremony. By the patriarchal law of visiting the sins of the fathers on the children, the tribe is to this day distinguished by the name of Kavarga (of the Ka class), Ka being the initial syllable of the Kanarese word Kullu (= thief).—*Mysore Census Report*, p. 235.

In Coorg there is a priestly class called Amma Kodaga or Kaveri Brahmans; but as they do not profess to follow any particular Veda, they are, properly speaking, no Brahmans. They are a very small community. With regard to them, Richter says:—

The Amma Kodagas live principally in the S.-W. parts of Coorg, and are the indigenous priesthood devoted to the worship of Amma the Kaveri goddess. They are of a quite unobtrusive character; do not intermarry with the other Coorgs, and are, generally speaking, inferior to them in personal appearance and strength of body. Their number is about 50, they are unlettered and devoid of Brahmanical lore. Their diet is vegetable food only, and they abstain from drinking liquor. Their complexion is rather fair, their eyes dark-brown, and their hair black and straight.—*Ethnological Compendium of the Castes and Tribes of Coorg*, by the Rev. G. Richter, p. 1.

---

[*] *Buchanan's Journey*, Vol. III, pp. 31, 16.

CHAP. X.—THE BRAHMANS OF KERALA, MALABAR, COCHIN AND TRAVANCORE.

The part of the western coast of the Deccan which extends from Cannanore and the Chandra Giri river on the north to Cape Comorin on the south, and which embraces at present the British district of Malabar, and the principalities of Cochin and Travancore, is, in many respects, a homogeneous tract distinguishable from every other part of India. This strip of country was called in ancient times Kerala or Chera, and governed by its own king. The language spoken by its people is Malaylan which, though allied to the Tamil, is a quite distinct dialect. The Nairs and the Namburi Brahmans, who form the chief elements in the population of Kerala, are not to be found in considerable numbers even in the adjoining districts of Coimbatore, Trichinopoly, Madura or Tinnevely. It is, however, the peculiar laws and customs of Kerala that distinguish it most from other parts of India. The very family type among the Nairs is so different from what is found in other countries, that it is very difficult for an outsider to form an idea of it. Among most of the nations throughout the world, each male member when he marries, becomes an unit of the society. During the lifetime of his father he may, with his wife, and in some cases with his children also, live under the parental roof. But each of the male members of the society is, in the eye of law, the centre of an independent group actual or possible. After his death, the usual rule is that his sons succeed to his property and his status, and every one traces his lineage in the male line, *i.e.*, in the line of his father, grandfather, great-grandfather, &c. The case among the Nairs is very different. Among them every girl is married formally when a child with a Brahman. But the titular husband can never claim her as his wife, and when she grows up she may choose any one, either of her own or of the Brahman caste, provided he is not a member of the same *tarwad* (the common residence of the children of the same maternal ancestor). A female member of a wealthy *tarwad* never leaves her maternal home, but is visited there by her husband. In the case of less wealthy *tarwads*, the women generally live with the husbands chosen by them. But in all cases the children succeed to the property and status of their mother's *tarwad*, and not to their male ancestors.

The marriage customs of the Namburi Brahmans of Malabar are not the same as those of the Nairs; nor are they quite identical with those of the Brahmans in other parts of India. In a Namburi family, it is only the eldest brother who is ordinarily allowed to take a wife by a regular marriage. If no male children be born to the eldest, then the brother next in rank may marry in the regular way, but not otherwise. The younger brothers, who are forbidden marriage, are allowed to form connexions with Ksatriya and Nair women.

The Namburis exact greater deference from the Sudras than the Brahmans in other parts of the country. A *Nair*, who is a high caste Sudra, may approach, but must not touch, a Namburi. A Tir, who is a cultivator by caste, has to remain thirty-six steps off from one ; a Malayaer hillman three or four steps further. A member of the degraded Puliyar caste has to keep himself at a distance of ninety-six steps. If a Puliyar touch a Brahman, the latter must make expiation by immediate bathing, and change of his Brahmanical thread.

The Namburis are, like most of the other classes of Deccani Brahmans, strict vegetarians. Their male members are allowed to eat with the Ksatriyas. The most striking peculiarity in a Namburi is the tuft of hair grown near the forehead, instead of the usual Brahmanical Sikha at the central part of the head. There are both Sivites and Vishnuvites among the Namburis. The former are called Chovar, the latter Panyon. The Namburi Brahmans seldom go abroad without holding a *chatra* or large umbrella. Their women also screen themselves with a *chatra* when they go out, which they do very seldom. The foreign Brahmans residing in Malabar are called Pattara. The Ambalvashis, who are the employés of the public shrines, are Namburis by descent, but degraded by their avocation.

The great Sankaracharya, whose name stands most conspicuous in the struggle for rooting out Buddhism from India, and who is regarded by Brahmans in every part of the country as an incarnation of Siva, was a Namburi.

PART V.
THE SEMI-BRAHMANICAL CASTES.

CHAP. I.—THE BHUINHAR BRAHMANS OF BEHAR AND BENARES.

THERE are various legends regarding the origin of this caste. The Bhuinhar Brahmans themselves claim to be true Brahmans descended from the rulers whom Parusu Ram set up in the place of the Ksatriya kings slain by him. The good Brahmans and the Ksatriyas of the country, however, look down upon them, and insinuate that they are of a mixed breed, the offspring of Brahman men and Ksatriya women. It is even said that the class was formed by the promotion of low caste men under the orders of a minister to a Raja who wanted a very large number of Brahmans to celebrate a religious ceremony, but for whom his minister could not procure the required number of true Brahmans. But this legendary theory is very strongly contradicted by the Aryan physiognomy of the Bhuinhars who, in respect of personal appearance, are in no way inferior to the Brahmans and the Rajputs. One of the most important points of difference between the Bhuinhar Brahmans, and the majority of the ordinary Brahmans is, that while the latter are divided into only those exogamous clans called Gotra, the former have among them, like the Rajputs, a twofold division based upon both Gotra and tribe. From this circumstance Mr. Risley[*] has been led to conclude that the Bhuinhar Brahmans are an offshoot of the Rajputs, and not true Brahmans. But as there are similar tribal divisions among the Maithila Brahmans of Tirhoot and the Saraswat Brahmans of the Panjab, it might, on the same ground, be said that the Saraswats and the Maithilas are offshoots of the Rajputs.

The theory that Bhuinhar Brahmans are an offshoot of the Rajputs, involves the utterly unfounded assumption that any of the military clans could have reason to be ashamed of their caste status. The 'royal race' had very good reasons to be proud of such surnames as Sinha, Roy and Thakoor, and it seems very unlikely that any of their clans could at any time be so foolish as to

---

[*] The grounds on which Mr. Risley rests his view will appear clear from the following extract:—

"An examination of the sections or exogamous groups into which the Babhans are divided appear, however, to tell strongly against the hypothesis that they are degraded Brahmans. These groups are usually the oldest and most durable element in the internal organisation of a caste or tribe, and may therefore be expected to offer the clearest indications as to its origin. Now we find among the Babhans section names of two distinct types, the one territorial referring either to some very early settlement of the section, or to the birthplace of its founder, and the other eponymous, the eponym being in most cases a Vedic Rishi or inspired sage. The names of the former class correspond to or closely resemble those current among Rajputs; the names of the latter are those of the standard Brahmanical Gotras. Where the matrimonial prohibitions based on these two classes of sections conflict, as must obviously often happen where every member of the caste necessarily belongs to both sets, the authority of the territorial class overrides that of the eponymous or Brahmanical class. Suppose, for instance, that a man of the Koronch territorial section and of the Sandilya eponymous section wishes to marry a woman of the Sakanwar territorial section, the fact that she also belongs to the Sandilya eponymous section will not operate as a bar to the marriage. Whatever may be the theory of the *purohits* of the caste, the Brahmanical Gotra is disregarded in practice. This circumstance seems to indicate that the territorial sections are the older of the two, and are probably the original sections of the caste, while the eponymous sections have been borrowed from the Brahmans in comparatively recent times. It would follow that the Babhans are an offshoot, not from the Brahmans, but from the Rajputs."—Risley's *Tribes and Castes*, Vol. I, Introduction.

club together for the purpose of assuming the Brahmanic surnames of Dobe, Tewari, Chobe and Upádhya. On the theory that the Bhuinhar Brahmans are an offshoot of the Rajputs, the clans that now profess to be Bhuinhar Rajputs are the residue that have stuck to their original status, and have never aspired to a higher one. But on this supposition it would be difficult to find any reason for the distinction between Bhuinhar Rajputs and the ordinary Rajputs.

The clue to the exact status of the Bhuinhar Brahmans is afforded by their very name. The word literally means a landholder. In the language of the Indian feudal system, *Bhum* is the name given to a kind of tenure similar to the *Inams* and *Jaigirs* of Mahomedan times. By a *Bhum*, according to the *Rajputana Gazetteer*, an hereditary, non-resumable and inalienable property in the soil was inseparably bound up with a revenue-free title. *Bhum* was given as compensation for bloodshed, in order to quell a feud, for distinguished services in the field, for protection of a border, or for the watch and ward of a village.* The tenure is very highly esteemed by Rajputs of all classes. The Maharajah of Kishengarh, the Thákoor of Fategarh, the Thákoor of Gunia, the Thákoor of Bandanwara, and the Thákoor of Tantoti are among the Bhumias of Ajmere. In Bengal the fact of the frontier districts of the east having been at one time under twelve Bhumia Kings is well known still by tradition.

The meaning of the designation Bhuinhar being as stated above, the Bhuinhar Brahmans are evidently those Brahmans who held grants of land for secular services. Whoever held a secular fief was a Bhuinhar. Where a Brahman held such a tenure he was called a Bhuinhar Brahman. Where the holder was a Ksatriya he was called a Bhuinhar Ksatriya. Bhuinhar Brah-

---

* The Assamese Bhuinhars do not wear the sacred thread, and do not claim to be either Brahmans or Ksatriyas.

mans are sometimes called simply Bhuinhars, just as the masons, whose class name in Bengali is *Raj mistri* (royal architect), are generally called *Raj*, which means a king.

In Assam the Bhuinhars hold their lands on very favourable terms; but no exceptional indulgence is shown to the Bhuinhars of Behar or Benares by the local zemindars. As may be expected the Bhuinhars are now chiefly an agricultural class; but like the good Brahmans, they never touch the plough. They will, however, do any kind of manual work except personal service. They serve not only as soldiers, constables, orderlies and gate-keepers, but also as porters, cartmen, and cutters of wood. Many of the Hindu cartmen and porters in Calcutta are Bhuinhars. Some of them are very proud and cantankerous. The fact that the Bhuinhars readily enlist in the army and in the police may be taken to show, to some extent, what their caste profession must have been in former times.

The Bhuinhars observe all their religious ceremonies in the same manner as the good Brahmans; but as they practise secular avocations they, like the Laukika Brahmans of Southern India, are not entitled to accept religious gifts, or to minister to any one as priests. The best Brahmans officiate as priests for the Bhuinhars, and it is not considered that they are degraded by doing so.

On the view that the Bhuinhars were anciently a fighting caste, it is not at all a matter for wonder that there are among them, as among the Rajputs, many big landholders. The Rajas named below are of the Bhuinhar caste :—

1. Raja of Benares.
2. Raja of Bettia in Champaran, North Behar.
3. Raja of Tikari in Gaya.
4. Raja of Hatwa in Saran, North Behar.
5. Raja of Tamakhi in Gorakpore.
6. Raja of Sheohar.
7. Raja of Maisadal in Midnapore, Bengal.
8. Raja of Pakour in Sonthal Pergunnahs, Bengal.
9. Raja of Moheshpore in Sonthal Pergunnahs, Bengal.

Like the Rajputs the Bhuinhar Brahmans form one great caste, and there are no sub-castes among them. They are divided into a large number of clans which, for purposes of marriage, are, with very few exceptions, all equal. The usual surnames of the Bhuinhar Brahmans are the same as those of the other Brahmans of Northern India. Being a fighting caste, a few of them have Rajput surnames.

CHAP. II.—THE BHATS AND THE CHARANAS.

The Bhats and the Charanas are very important castes in Rajputana and the adjoining provinces. They are the minstrels, historians and genealogists of the Rajput chiefs, and are very much feared by their constituents, as it is in their power to lower any family by distorting history. They all take the holy thread, and as their persons are considered to be sacred by all classes, they seem to have been originally Brahmans. The very name of Bhatta points also to the same conclusion, as it means a learned man, and is an honorific surname of many of the best families of Brahmanas in every part of the country. In all probability the Bhats are the caste who were usually employed by the Rajput princes in diplomatic service, while the Charanas, as their very name indicates, were the spies. At any rate this view not only explains the fact that the Bhats have a higher caste status than the Charanas, but is supported also by the custom which still prevails among the Rajputs of employing the Bhats to conduct negotiations for marriage alliances.

Sir John Malcolm gives the following account of the Bhats :—

The Bhats or Raos seldom sacrifice themselves; but as chroniclers or bards, they share power, and sometimes office with the Charanas. Among the Bhilalas and lower tribes they enjoy great and exclusive influence; they give praise and fame in their songs to those who are liberal to them, while they visit those who neglect or injure them, with satires, in which they usually reproach them with spurious birth and inherent meanness. Sometimes the Bhat, if very seriously offended, fixes the figure of the person he desires to degrade on a long pole, and appends to it a slipper as a mark of disgrace. In such cases the song of the Bhat records the infamy of the object of his revenge. This image usually travels the country till the party or his friends purchase the cessation of the ridicule and curses thus entailed. It is not deemed in these countries in the power of a prince, much less any other person, to stop a Bhat, or even punish him for such a proceeding: he is protected by the superstitious and religious awe which, when general among a people, controls even despotism.—Malcolm's *Central India*, Vol. II, Chap. XIV, pp. 113-114.

The poetic castes in fact performed the functions of the *tiers-état* in Rajasthan, and the privilege of commenting on the actions of their Kings, which they possessed and very often abused, was very nearly unlimited. In Rajputana there are many big landholders and men of influence among the Bhats and the Charanas; but there are very few Sanskritists among them. The usual surname of the Bhats is Rao. They are divided into two classes, namely, the Brahma Bhats and the Yoga Bhats. The former are poets and minstrels who recount, in verse, the history of the great Rajput heroes, ancient and modern. The Yoga Bhats are the genealogists. The Bhats of Bengal are mere beggars, without regular constituents, and without the slightest pretension of poetic capacity. On the occasions of Pujas and Shradhas in the houses of the rich, they present themselves uninvited, and make such a horrid uproar by shouting and singing, that the master of the house besieged by them is glad to pay something to get rid of them. If refused, they will get to the top of a tree or wall, and threaten to commit suicide by falling headlong on the ground. Being thus terrorised the ladies of the house insist upon their immediate dismissal anyhow, and it is therefore quite impossible to avoid submitting to their exactions on ceremonial occasions. With regard to the Charanas Sir John Malcolm gives the following account:—

They are divided into two tribes, the Kachili who are merchants, and the Maru who are bards. These again branch out into one hundred and twenty other tribes, many of whom are the descendants in the female line of Brahmans and Rajputs. They are taught to read and write, and the class who traffic (generally in camels and horses) are shrewd men of business; while the Maru Charanas apply their skill to the genealogy of tribes, and to the recital of numerous legends (usually in verse), celebrating the praises of former heroes, which it is their duty to chant, to gratify the pride and rouse the emulation of their descendants. The Charana's chief power is derived from an impression that it is certain ruin and destruction to shed his blood, or that of any of his family, or to be the cause of its being shed. They obtain a high rank in society, and a certain livelihood, from the superstitious belief which they are educated to inculcate, and which they teach their children to consider as their chief object in life to maintain. A Charana becomes the safeguard of travellers and security for merchants, and his bond is often preferred among the Rajputs, when rents and property are concerned, to that of the wealthiest bankers. When he trades himself, he alone is trusted and trusts among the community to which he belongs. The Charana who accompanies travellers likely to be attacked by Rajput robbers, when he sees the latter approach, warns them off by holding a dagger in his hand, and if they do not attend to him, he stabs himself in a place that is not mortal, and taking the blood from the wound, throws it at the assailants with imprecations of future woe and ruin. If this has not the desired effect, the wounds are repeated, and in extreme cases one of the Charana's relations, commonly a female child or an old woman, is made a sacrifice. The same process is adopted to enforce the payment of a debt to himself or a claim for which he has become security. It is not unusual, as the next step, to slay himself; and the catastrophe has been known to close in the voluntary death of his wives and children. The females of the Charanas are distinct from all the other population, both in dress and manners. They often reside in separate villages, and the traveller is surprised to see them come out in their long robes, and attend him for some space, chanting his welcome to their abode. The Charanas are not only treated by the Rajputs with great respect (the highest rulers of that race rising when one of this class enters or leaves an assembly), but they have more substantial marks of regard. When they engage in trade, lighter duties are collected from them than others. They receive at all feasts and marriages presents that are only limited by the ability of the parties. The evil consequences of a Charana being driven to undergo a violent death, can be alone averted by grants of land and costly gifts to surviving relations; and the Rajput chief, whose guilt is recorded (for all these sacrifices are subjects of rude poems), as the cause of such sacred blood being shed, is fortunate when he can by any means have his repentance and generosity made part of the legend.—Malcolm's *Central India*, Vol. II, Chap. XIV, p. 108 *et seq.*

About the peregrinations of the Bhats and the Charanas, and the periodical visits paid by them to their constituents, a graphic account is to be found in the following extract :—

When the rainy season closes, and travelling becomes practicable, the bard sets off on his yearly tour from his residence in the Bhatwara of some city or town. One by one he visits each of the Rajput chiefs who are his patrons, and from whom he has received portions of land, or annual grants of money, timing his arrival, if possible, to suit occasions of marriage or other domestic festival. After he has received the usual courtesies, he produces the 'Bahi,' a book written in his own crabbed hieroglyphics, or in those of his fathers, which contains the descent of the house; if the chief be the Tilayet or head of the family, from the founder of the tribe; if he be a Phatayo, or cadet, from the immediate ancestor of the branch, interspersed with many a verse or ballad, the dark sayings contained in which are chanted forth in musical cadence to a delighted audience, and are then orally interpreted by the bard, with many an illustrative anecdote or tale. The 'Bahi' is not, however, merely a source for the gratification of family pride, or even of love of song; it is also a record of authority by which questions of consanguinity are determined when marriage is on the *tapis*, and disputes relating to the division of ancestral property are decided. It is the duty of a bard at each periodical visit to register the births, marriages and deaths which have taken place in the family since his last circuit, as well as to chronicle all other events worthy of remark which have occurred to affect the fortunes of his patron; nor have we ever heard even a doubt suggested regarding the accurate, much less the honest, fulfilment of this duty by the bard.—Forbes's *Ras Mala*, Vol. II, pp. 263-64.

PART VI.
THE DEGRADED BRAHMANS.

PRELIMINARY REMARKS.

There are various classes of degraded Brahmans who now form, more or less completely, separate castes. Their social ostracism is due to one or other of the following causes:—

1. Alleged intercourse with Mahomedans at some by-gone period.
2. Ministering to the low castes as priests.
3. Being connected with the great public shrines.
4. Accepting forbidden gifts.
5. Ministering as priests at a cremation.
6. Being suspected to be of spurious birth.
7. By being tillers of the soil.
8. By menial service.

CHAP. I.—THE HOSAINIS AND KUVACHANDAS.

Hosainis.—These are a class of Brahmans to be found in many parts of Western India, and especially near Ahmednagar. They have actually adopted to some extent the Mahomedan faith and its observances, though they retain some of the Brahmanic practices too, and generally intermarry only among themselves. As a class they have no importance. They are chiefly beggars.

Kuvachandas—Found in Sind, and they generally resemble the Mussalmans in their habits.

CHAP. II.—THE PIRALI TAGORES OF CALCUTTA.

OF the several classes degraded by alleged intercourse with Mahomedans, the Pirālis of Bengal are the most important from many points of view. They claim to be a section of the Radriya Brahmans of the country with whom alone they intermarry, though such alliance is always very expensive to them. The good Radriya who marries into a Pirāli family is himself reduced to the rank of a Pirāli, and always demands a heavy premium as a *sine quâ non*. With the exception of the family of Babu Debendra Nath Tagore who are Brahmos, the Pirālis are very orthodox Hindus. The following account relating to the degradation of Purushottama, the ancestor of the clan, is given by one of their leading members, the late Honorable Prasanna Kumar Tagore, C.S.I.:—

Purushottama was called Pirāli for having married the daughter of a person blemished in caste. According to the books of the Ghattaks, Janaki Ballabha and Kamdeva Roy Chowdri, inhabitants of Gurgain, in Pergana Chengutia, brought a suit against an ancestor of Sri Kanta Roy, of Jessore. An Amin, named *Pirāli Khan*, was deputed by the zemindar for the purpose of holding an investigation into the case. There was an altercation between the Amin and some of the inhabitants of the place as to whether the smell of a thing was tantamount to half-eating it. Some time after the said Pirāli Khan invited several persons all of whom lost their caste, as he made them smell forbidden food. *Janaki Ballabha* and *Kamadeva* having sat near the Amin and been reported to have eaten the food, became Mahomedans, under the names of *Jamal Khan* and *Kamal Khan*, pursuant to the decision of the Pandits of those times. Their descendants, *Arjuna Khan, Dinanath Khan, &c.*, live like Mahomedans up to this day in Magura and Basundia,

Pergana *Chengutia*, zillah Jessore. They form their connections by marriage with the Khan Chowdries of Broome, but not with any other Mahomedans. The remaining persons present on the occasion were called Pirāli. Purushottama was one of the latter. Others give a different account. They say that when Purushottama was in Jessore, on his way to bathe in the Ganges, the Chowdries of that place, who became polluted in the above mentioned way, forcibly took him to their house with a view to give him a daughter of theirs in marriage. Seeing that the bride was very beautiful, Purushottama agreed to marry her. After this marriage, Purushottama left the original seat of his family and settled in Jessore. Purushottama had a son named Balarama. Panchanana, the fifth in descent from Balarama left Jessore and came to *Govindpore*, the site of Fort William, where he purchased land, and built thereon a dwelling-house and a temple. His son Jairam was employed as an Amin in the settlement of the 24-Pergunnahs and discharged his duties with considerable credit. At the capture of Calcutta he is said to have lost all his property with the exception of Rs. 13,000 in cash.

Jairam's house was taken by the English for the purpose of building Fort William. He received some money and land as compensation, and removed himself to Pathuriaghata. He died in the year 1762, leaving four sons, named Ananda Ram, Nilmani, Darpa Narayan and Govinda. The eldest, Ananda Ram, was the first who received a liberal English education. His family and that of his youngest brother, who superintended the building of the Fort William, have become extinct. Nilmani was the grandfather of Dwarkanath Tagore, who occupied a foremost rank in the society of his day. See S. C. Bose's *Hindus as they are*, pp. 171—74.

With reference to the above, it may be observed here that the alleged enjoyment of the smell of a Mahomedan's savoury meat, cannot, by itself, explain the perpetual degradation of Purushottama, or of any of the other guests of Pirāli. The sin of even voluntary and actual eating of such food is not an inexpiable one, and there is not within the four corners of the Shastras, any such utterly unreasonable and Draconian law as would visit a man with eternal degradation for involuntarily inhaling the smell of forbidden food. There are also other inherent improbabilities in the story as narrated above. Unless the Amin, and the inhabitants of the locality where he was conducting his investigations, were quite demented, there could not possibly be an occasion for any altercation between the parties as to a question of the Hindu's religion. Then, again, if the habits and prejudices of the Hindus in those times be taken into consideration, it would seem quite impossible that Pirāli would have invited any number of them to his house, or that they would have responded to the invitation so far as to enter his dining-room. Hindus and Mahomedans very often exchange visits for ceremonial and official purposes. But even when they are on the most friendly terms, a man professing the one religion will not ask a votary of the other to sit by his table while he is at dinner. The orthodox Hindu's prejudices are such that after sitting on the same carpet with a Mahomedan or a Christian friend, or shaking hands with such a person, he has to put off his clothes, and to bathe or sprinkle his person with the holy water of the Ganges. The Mahomedan gentleman of the country who know well of these prejudices on the part of their Hindu fellow-countrymen, therefore, never ask them to mix too familiarly, and the Hindus also keep themselves at a sufficient distance to avoid that they must regard as contaminations. The dwelling-house of every native of India, be he a Hindu or a Mahomedan, consists of two parts, namely, the *zenana* and the *boytakhana*. The *zenana* apartments are reserved for the ladies, and the dining-rooms for the members of the house are always within the *zenana*. The *boytakhana* is the outer part of the house where visitors are received. The Mussalmans do sometimes entertain their co-religionists in the *boytakhana;* but no orthodox Hindu would enter such a place while the plates are in it, or would remain there a moment after any sign of preparations for introducing any kind of cooked eatables.

From what is stated above, it would appear that the causes assigned by the Pirālis themselves for their degradation cannot satisfactorily account for their status in the Hindu caste system. From the general tenor of their story, it seems more probable that Purushottama was an officer in the staff of the surveyor, Pirāli, and that, as Amīns and their underlings usually do, he made himself very unpopular among his co-religionists by attempting to invade the titles to their patrimony, so as to lead them to club together for ostracising him on the allegation that he had tasted or smelt forbidden food.

The reason why the Pirālis left their original habitat, and settled in Calcutta, is not far to seek. Purushottama who was first outcasted had evidently made his native village too hot for him. He removed to Jessore; but even at Jessore he could not have, in his degraded condition, found many friends. His descendant, Panchanana, therefore removed to Calcutta in search of employment, and a place where he could live in peace. Calcutta was then practically ruled by the East India Company, who had no reason whatever to pay any regard to any rule or decree of caste discipline. The majority of the well-to-do population of Calcutta were then of the weaver caste, with a sprinkling of Sonar Banyas and Kāyasthas. Good Brahmans visited the towns sometimes for ministering to their disciples or collecting the donations of the rich Sudras to their *toles* or Sanskrit schools. But those were days when the orthodox and respectable Brahmans of Bengal considered it beneath their dignity to engage in secular pursuits, and even to those who were inclined to pocket their pride for the sake of pelf, the service of the East India Company could not then have much attraction. Whatever the cause might have been, the Brahmanic population of Calcutta was not very large in its early days. When such was the state of things Panchanana settled in it. A Brahman is a Brahman though outcasted by his clansmen. The Sonar Banyas of Calcutta were themselves outcastes, and as for the Tantis and Kāyasthas, they could have neither the motive nor the power to subject the outcaste Panchanana to any kind of persecution. The Setts and the Malliks actually befriended his family, though apparently without recognizing their status as Brahmans so far as to accept their hospitality in any shape. In Prasanna Kumar Tagore's account of his family history it is stated that Ram Krishna Mallik exchanged turbans with his ancestor Darpa Narain. That was no doubt a sign of friendship, but not of the kind of veneration which Banyas must have for good Brahmans. It is said however that for nearly half a century after the arrival of their ancestor, Panchanana, in Calcutta, the Pirālis were recognized as good Brahman. But when they became wealthy and influential, the late Babu Durga Charan Mukerji, of Bag Bazar, formed a party for degrading them. Perhaps some of the Kāyastha magnates of Calcutta secretly supported Durga Charan in persecuting the Pirālis.

The way in which the Tagores of the last century attained their wealth is not well known. Panchanana's son Jairam, by serving as an Amin for the survey and settlement of the villages acquired by the East India Company under the charter of Emperor Ferokshere, apparently laid a substantial foundation. His youngest son Govinda, who superintended the building of Fort William, presumably improved the patrimony materially. Darpa Narain, the third son of Jairam and the great-grandfather of Sir Maharaja Jotindra Mohan, held for some time a high office in the service of the French East India Company. Nilmoni, the second son of Jairam and the grandfather of the celebrated Dwarka Nath Tagore, did not inherit any share of the family estate. But he was befriended by one of the Sonar Banaiya millionaires of his time, and was enabled by his friend to build a separate house for his residence on the site now occupied by the palatial mansion belonging to his descendants. Nilmoni's second son, Ram Moni, served as a clerk in the Police Court. Dwarka Nath, the second son of Ram Moni, made himself wealthy and famous in various ways. He began his career by entering the service of the Government of Bengal in the Salt Department.

About the beginning of the present century when the estates of most of the great zemindars of Bengal were brought to sale, for arrears of revenue, the Pirāli Tagores bought many valuable properties, and became themselves great zemindars. The total income of the several branches of the Tagore family must at present be more than £100,000. The leading members of the clan in the last generation were Dwarka Nath Tagore, Prasunna Kumar Tagore and Ramanath Tagore. Among the living celebrities of the family, Maharaja Sir Jotindra Mohun Tagore is deservedly esteemed as one of its brightest ornaments. He was a member of the Legislative Council of India for several years, and the British Government of India has conferred upon him every possible title of honour at its disposal. His brother Maharaja Sourendra Mohan Tagore is a votary of the science of music, but at the same time has been steadily improving his estate by efficient management like his illustrious brother. Dwarka Nath's son Devendra Nath is now in "sear and yellow leaf" of life. On account of his devotion to religion he is usually called a Maharshi or Saint. His son Satyendra Nath is the first Hindu member of the Indian Civil Service, and is now employed as a District Judge in the Bombay Presidency. Babu Kali Krishna Tagore, who represents another branch, does not move much in Calcutta society; but next to Sir J. M. Tagore, he is perhaps the richest member of the family.

From a long time the Tagores have been struggling hard to be restored to caste. Ward says that Raja Krishna Chundra of Nadiya was promised one lac of rupees by a Pirāli, if he would only honour him with a visit for a few minutes, but he refused. Similar offers, though of smaller amounts, have been again and again made to the great Pandits of Nadiya, but have been similarly declined. But the Tagores are now fast rising in the scale of caste. Poor Brahmans now more or less openly accept their gifts, and sometimes even their hospitality; and Sir J. M. Tagore is on the way towards acquiring an influence on the Pandits which may one day enable him to re-establish his family completely in caste.

CHAP. III.—THE BARNA BRAHMANS.

THE Brahmans that minister to the low Sudra castes and outcastes, are looked upon as degraded persons, and they generally form separate castes. The good Brahmans will not take even a drink of water from their hands, and intermarriage between them is quite out of the question. In Bengal the following classes of Sudras and outcastes have special priests :—

1. Sonar Vaniya—Gold merchants.
2. Goala—Cowherds.
3. Kalu—Oilmen.
4. Dhopa—Washermen.
5. Bagdi—Aboriginal tribe of woodcutters and fishermen.
6. Kaibarta.

The priests of each of these classes form independent castes, without the right of intermarriage or dining together with any other section of the Brahmanic caste. With the exception of a few of the Sonar Vaniya Brahmans, these Barna Brahmans, as they are called, are mostly very poor, and utterly without any kind of social position. The priests of the Kaibartas are in some places called Vyasokta Brahmans.

§ 2.—*Barna Brahmans of Mithila.*

The following castes of Mithila have special Brahmans :—

Tatwa—Weaver.
Teli—Oilman.
Kasara—Brazier.
Sonar—Goldsmith.

§ 3.—*Barna Brahmans of Gujrat and Rajputana.*

The following are regarded as Barna Brahmans in Gujrat, and have a low caste status :—

> Abhira Brahmans—Priests of the cowherd caste.
> Kunbi Gour—Priests of the Kunbis.
> Gujara Gour—Priests of the Gujars.
> Machi Gour—Priests of the Machi or fishermen.
> Gandharpa Gour—Priests of the musicians.
> Koli Gour—Priests of the Kolis.
> Garudyas—Priests of the Chamhars and Dheds.

§ 4.—*Barna Brahmans of Telingana.*

The following are the names of the classes of Tailangi Brahmans that minister to the low castes :—

> 1. Ganda Dravidras.
> 2. Nambi Varlu.

§ 5.—*Barna Brahmans of Malabar.*

> 1. Eledus—Priests of the Nairs.

CHAP. IV.—THE BRAHMANS CONNECTED WITH THE GREAT PUBLIC SHRINES.

Of the Brahmans who are considered as having a very low status on account of their being connected with the great public shrines, the following classes are the most important :—

1. Gayalis of Gaya.
2. Chowbays of Muttra.
3. Pukar Sevaks of Pushkar.
4. Ganga Putras of Benares.
5. Pandas of Orissa.
6. Pandarams of Southern India.
7. Prayagwalas of Prayag or Allahabad.
8. Divas—connected with the Ballavachari shrines of Western India.
9. Moylars—connected with the Madhava temples of Tulava; said to be of spurious birth.
10. Ambalavasis—connected with the shrines in Malabar.
11. Numbi Brahmans—connected with the public shrines of Karnata.

Most of these classes are very rich, but utterly illiterate. Mere residence in a place of pilgrimage, for a few generations, tends to lower the status of a family. The Bengali Brahmans settled at Benares are called by their clansmen Kashials, and looked down upon as men whose birth is spurious, or as being in the habit of earning their livelihood by accepting forbidden gifts. The Brahmans of Southern India also look down upon their clansmen permanently residing in Benares, without any connection with their native country.*

---

*The reader may have some idea of this feeling from the following passage in Mr. Wilkin's *Modern Hinduism* :—
A few months ago, when travelling on the East India Railway,

The Somparas connected with the shrine of Somnath seem to have a higher position than the priests of the public shrines usually have. There is a class of Brahmans in the Doab who call themselves Chowbays of Mathura, but have nothing to do with priestly work. These are very high class Brahmans. There are many learned Sanskritists and English scholars among them. Some of them hold high offices in the service of Government and also of the Native States. One of the greatest of these is Kumar Jwala Prasad, who is at present the District Judge of Azimgarh. His father, Raja Jai Kishen, rendered eminent services to the Government at the time of the Sepoy Mutiny, and is still employed as a Deputy Collector. Another member of the Chowbay caste, named Raghu Nath Das, is the Prime Minister of Kota.

I met with two Brahmans from Mysore. They are educated men; one of them was expecting to appear in the following B. A. Examination of the Madras University. When we were leaving Benares, it occurred to me to ask if they had any friends in that holy city. They said,—"No, but we soon found some Brahmans from our part of the country." I said "oh, then you were well received and hospitably entertained by them of course?" I shall never forget the look of infinite disdain with which one of them replied: "Do you think we would eat with men who live in such a city as Benares, and associate with Brahmans of this district? No, we contented ourselves whilst there with one meal a day, which we cooked for ourselves." My question appeared to them about as reasonable as if I had asked a nobleman in England if he had dined with scavenger.—Wilkin's *Modern Hinduism*, pp. 163 164.

www.ingramcontent.com/pod-product-compliance
Lightning Source LLC
Chambersburg PA
CBHW030353170426
43202CB00010B/1364